Stitching Truth

WOMEN'S PROTEST ART
IN PINOCHET'S CHILE

SERIES EDITORS

Adam Strom & the Facing History and Ourselves Staff

PRIMARY WRITER

Dan Eshet

With an introduction by Marjorie Agosín
Luella La Mer Slaner Professor of
Latin American Studies at Wellesley College

FACING
HISTORY
AND
OURSELVES

Facing History and Ourselves is an international educational and professional development organization whose mission is to engage students of diverse backgrounds in an examination of racism, prejudice, and antisemitism in order to promote the development of a more humane and informed citizenry. By studying the historical development of the Holocaust and other examples of genocide, students make the essential connection between history and the moral choices they confront in their own lives. For more information about Facing History and Ourselves, please visit our website at *www.facinghistory.org.*

ISBN-13: 978-0-9798440-2-7

ISBN-10: 0-9798440-2-9

Facing History and Ourselves Headquarters
16 Hurd Road
Brookline, MA 02445-6919

FACING
HISTORY
AND
OURSELVES

ABOUT FACING HISTORY AND OURSELVES

Facing History and Ourselves is a nonprofit educational organization whose mission is to engage students of diverse backgrounds in an examination of racism, prejudice, and antisemitism in order to promote a more humane and informed citizenry. As the name Facing History and Ourselves implies, the organization helps teachers and their students make the essential connections between history and the moral choices they confront in their own lives, and offers a framework and a vocabulary for analyzing the meaning and responsibility of citizenship and the tools to recognize bigotry and indifference in their own worlds. Through a rigorous examination of the failure of democracy in Germany during the 1920s and '30s and the steps leading to the Holocaust, along with other examples of hatred, collective violence, and genocide in the past century, Facing History and Ourselves provides educators with tools for teaching history and ethics, and for helping their students learn to combat prejudice with compassion, indifference with participation, myth and misinformation with knowledge.

Believing that no classroom exists in isolation, Facing History and Ourselves offers programs and materials to a broad audience of students, parents, teachers, civic leaders, and all of those who play a role in the education of young people. Through significant higher education partnerships, Facing History and Ourselves also reaches and impacts teachers before they enter their classrooms.

By studying the choices that led to critical episodes in history, students learn how issues of identity and membership, ethics and judgment have meaning today and in the future. Facing History and Ourselves' resource books provide a meticulously researched yet flexible structure for examining complex events and ideas. Educators can select appropriate readings and draw on additional resources available online or from our comprehensive lending library.

Our foundational resource book, Facing History and Ourselves: Holocaust and Human Behavior, embodies a sequence of study that begins with identity—first individual identity and then group and national identities, with their definitions of membership. From there the program examines the failure of democracy in Germany and the steps leading to the Holocaust—the most documented case of twentieth-century indifference, de-humanization, hatred, racism, antisemitism, and mass murder. It goes on to explore difficult questions of judgment, memory, and legacy, and the necessity for responsible participation to prevent injustice. Facing History and Ourselves then returns to the theme of civic participation to examine stories of individuals, groups, and nations who have worked to build just and inclusive communities and whose stories illuminate the courage, compassion, and political will that are needed to protect democracy today and in generations to come. Other examples in which civic dilemmas test democracy, such as the Armenian Genocide and the U.S. civil rights movement, expand and deepen the connection between history and the choices we face today and in the future.

Facing History and Ourselves has offices or resource centers in the United States, Canada, and the United Kingdom as well as in-depth partnerships in Rwanda, South Africa, and Northern Ireland. Facing History and Ourselves' outreach is global, with educators trained in more than 80 countries and delivery of our resources through a website accessed worldwide with online content delivery, a program for international fellows, and a set of NGO partnerships. By convening conferences of scholars, theologians, educators, and journalists, Facing History and Ourselves' materials are kept timely, relevant, and responsive to salient issues of global citizenship in the twenty-first century.

For more than 30 years, Facing History and Ourselves has challenged students and educators to connect the complexities of the past to the moral and ethical issues of today. They explore democratic values and consider what it means to exercise one's rights and responsibilities in the service of a more humane and compassionate world. They become aware that "little things are big"—seemingly minor decisions can have a major impact and change the course of history.

For more about Facing History and Ourselves, visit our website at *www.facinghistory.org*.

The Arpillerista

The arpillerista,
artisan of remains
burns with rage and cold
as she tenderly
picks through the remnants of her dead,
salvages the shroud of her husband
the trousers left after the absences
submerges herself in cloth of foaming, silent blood
and though she is fragile she grows large,
sovereign over her adobe hut,
her ragged scraps
and determined to tell her story
truer than the tale woven by her sister Philomena.

Disruptive and beautiful she
puts together her flayed remnants
like a greenish forgotten skin
and with her disguised thimble
hidden in the pocket of her modest apron
and her harmless needle
she conjures up victorious armies
embroiders humble people smiling, become triumphant
brings the dead back to life
fabricates water, bell towers, schools, dining rooms
giant suns
and the Cordillera of the Andes
peaks opening like portals
of this splendid city.

—Marjorie Agosín
Scraps of Life: Chilean Arpilleras

Contents

*Lesson plans that accompany this publication are available at **www.facinghistory.org**.*

FOREWORD

Adam Strom
Director of Research and Development, Facing History and Ourselves

Stitching Truth: Women's Protest Art in Pinochet's Chile is one of the first case studies in Facing History and Ourselves' Making History Series. Like all of our materials, it is embedded in what we call the scope and sequence of our program. Our resources and seminars begin with an examination of individual and group identities and move to a study of historical examples of racism, antisemitism, and intolerance before confronting questions of judgment and responsibility, memory, and civic participation. These resources and seminars help teachers and students explore historical dilemmas and make connections to their own lives with the hope of finding ways to strengthen the foundations of democracy.

Our teachers and students tell us that they want to make a positive difference, and yet many report feeling powerless and unable to make an impact on the world around them. Yet, without people standing up and effecting change, inequity and injustice remain unchallenged. In an interview with Facing History and Ourselves Executive Director Margot Stern Strom, journalist Bill Moyers explains that the health of a democracy depends on an active citizenry:

> The problem of democracy is the problem of the individual citizen who takes himself or herself lightly historically. . . . By that I mean if you do not believe that you can

make a difference, you're not going to try to make a difference, you're not going to try to matter, and you will leave it to someone else who may or may not do what is in the best interest of your values or of democracy's values.[1]

For many people the challenge is not only about wanting to make a difference, it is also about finding a way to get involved. Raquel F., a student in a Facing History and Ourselves class at International High School in Queens, New York, described her dilemma:

> My father has been in Rwanda several times since the genocide helping people to rebuild. I'm not sure that I am ready to take those risks and sometimes I wonder how and where I can help. I try to keep in mind what journalist Bill Moyers said: "You can't do everything at one time, but you can do something at once."[2]

The question "How can I make a difference?" was echoed by a teacher attending a Facing History and Ourselves seminar in Bogotá, Colombia—a country struggling to overcome a long history of violence. "What choices," she asked, "do people really have when they live in a state of terror?" *Stitching Truth: Women's Protest Art in Pinochet's Chile* offers insight into her difficult question by focusing on a group of

---

1 Bill Moyers, *Interview with Margot Strom*, VHS, April 1, 1986 (Brookline: Facing History and Ourselves, 1986).

2 Facing History and Ourselves, *1996 New York Benefit Dinner*, VHS (Brookline: Facing History and Ourselves, 1996).

marginalized women, many of them poor and illiterate, who stood up to a dictator and helped to restore democracy to their country.

The story of the sisters, wives, and mothers who made up the women's protest movement in Chile during Pinochet's dictatorship (1973–1990) is an incredible story of courage and resistance. Facing what would seem like insurmountable odds, the women challenged silence and terror imposed by Pinochet, his military, and his secret police. With the help of the Catholic archbishop of Santiago, the women stitched together scraps of fabric into *arpilleras* (colorful tapestries that document the abuses of the Pinochet dictatorship) and turned those arpilleras into a nonviolent weapon against the regime. An extraordinary combination of personal determination and courage propelled these women, the *arpilleristas*, into a leading role in the movement to restore democracy to Chile.

This case study is told in several parts. It begins with a reflection on the arpilleristas and the women's protest movement in Chile by award-winning scholar, poet, and activist Marjorie Agosín. The introduction is followed by several readings comprising a historical narrative that describes the movement and a series of primary source documents, including poetry, diplomatic correspondence, and, of course, photographs of the arpilleras themselves. Each section of the case study is sharpened by "Connections" questions that are designed to stimulate students' reflections and to offer additional resources. On our website, *www.facinghistory.org*, teachers will find a series of comprehensive lesson plans that offer exciting ways to use the case study in the classroom.

The development of this case study has been a team process that included Facing History and Ourselves staff and scholars from outside the organization. Each of them deserves recognition. Dan Eshet is the primary writer of the case study. Fran Colletti introduced all of us at Facing History to the work of the arpilleristas and worked with Marjorie Agosín to dream of ways to bring these magnificent stories and weavings into classrooms. Agosín wrote the introduction and we are indebted to her for her scholarship, poetry, tireless activism, and generosity. She also introduced us to Peter Winn and Peter Kornbluh, who reviewed our text and offered criticism, additional information, and insights. Margot Stern Strom, Marc Skvirsky, Marty Sleeper, and Karen Murphy all made important contributions to this work and made sure that this case study is in line with Facing

> **The problem of democracy is the problem of the individual citizen who takes himself or herself lightly . . . .**

History and Ourselves' pedagogy and educational goals. Jennifer Gray diligently researched the documents and images that illustrate this work. Nicole Breaux managed the publication of this project with Robert Lavelle. Elisabeth Kanner wrote the lesson plans that accompany this case study. I would also like to thank Sam Gilbert for his thoughtful suggestions as a copyeditor. Last, Books By Design, Inc., copyedited, proofread, and put together the design components of the final version of the text.

INTRODUCTION

Majorie Agosín
Luella La Mer Slaner Professor of Latin American Studies at Wellesley College,
an award-winning poet, and a human rights activist

During the early years of the Chilean military dictatorship, the city of Santiago always seemed dark and silent. A curfew forced the people to return to their homes at night and remain inside until the following day. I remember the days too. I remember the sunny squares of Santiago and how they became empty, just like its many gardens where children once played and laughed. In the empty plaza, all one could hear was the wind from the Andes and the sound of heavy boots patrolling the streets. I often dreamt of a night without fear and without a curfew. My city, once open and filled with noises, was now still and somber.

> **It felt as if each person lived trapped in her or his own silence, as if the city were turning into one perpetual night of shadows.**

The rule of General Augusto Pinochet plunged the country into a culture of terror and fear. It felt as if each person lived trapped in her or his own silence, as if the city were turning into one perpetual night of shadows.

While most of the population was living this internal exile, some Chileans created a different sort of life, one that was not shaped by the demands of Pinochet's government. Secretly, groups of intellectuals gathered in homes to talk about books that had been banned and censored. The meetings lasted from the beginning of curfew until it was lifted the following day. There were also women's groups that formed literary workshops to resist succumbing to fear. They refused to play active roles in a society that punished its artists, banning their books and burning them. Poetry, once so vibrant and alive, was written in secret: it had become a dangerous activity. Yet people wrote on napkins, on shoeboxes, and poets recited subversive poems in public buses. Life was still possible in the surreal world of order and punishment that the generals had created.

Pía Barros, a remarkable writer and a friend of mine, created a series of workshops all around Santiago, encouraging women to gather in their houses to talk and write about the dreadful state of the nation. Churches also provided safe havens for this parallel existence. For me, these gatherings provided a powerful inner light that served to remind me of our humanity, of our ability to think and contest the everyday horrors of life in a dictatorship.

Chilean *arpilleras*—the apparently simple embroidered fabrics that narrate the darker, otherwise censored acts of the Pinochet regime—belong to this other life that existed in Chile. I had the chance to get to know some of the women who made them. Marginalized by poverty and sexism, they carried on tenaciously with their work during this dark era. They turned their sorrow into a unique art form that recounted, through hand-sewn images, their lives as mothers in search of their missing children, as civilians demanding truth and justice.

The arpilleras were created as a response to censorship, as a way to fight against the impunity enjoyed by government forces. They became an important vehicle for spreading the news about Chile's situation. These pieces of cloth traveled abroad: customs officials never suspected that these humble wall hangings had the power to transform those who touched them. The arpilleras made it to museums around the world, to the calendars of Amnesty International, to the homes of exiles, and to many others who cared deeply about Chile.

The women who started this arpillera movement began their journey in the places of fear—hospitals, morgues, and cemeteries. They told me how they would recognize one of their own: each carried a mark of pain. They would ask each other whether they were there for a vanished son or a husband and how many children had been taken, when they had disappeared. Violeta Morales, one of the founders of the movement, always said that she was able to recognize her own grief in the faces of others. And they recognized the shoes worn out from walking the streets in search of their loved ones.

Their first conversations were heavy with the language of pain, but the exchanges quickly turned into a language of solidarity. Slowly, they began to think of ways of uniting in a collective project that would transcend their individual plights. Soon they gained the support of the Vicariate of Solidarity, a branch of the Catholic Church. This organization, under the direction of Cardinal Silva Henríquez, a noted human rights activist, was created to protect the country's victims.

The arpilleras are made with plain scraps of cloth; they are made with the fabrics of scarcity. From marginality, these beautiful tapestries emerge, describing through their embroidered images daily life under Pinochet. Many show the abduction of young people, torture, arbitrary detention, fear, even exile. In other words, the arpilleras are an artistic and historical record of human rights violations, a record virtually unthinkable at a time of suffocating censorship. As a counterpoint to the images of loss and absence, some chronicle the history of Chile before Pinochet. These are moving arpilleras set against a landscape of hope, where scenes of families sharing a convivial meal contrast with more sedate images of family gatherings haunted by an empty seat, the seat of the disappeared loved one who will never come home. If Latin American military dictatorships inspired terror by destroying lives, women's movements attempted to honor life, to celebrate life, to preserve—through quilts and other domestic crafts—the memory of lives snatched away.

I also recall the arpillera at the center of which Violeta Morales placed an enormous dove; or the ones by Viviana Díaz, which always included a table with flowers and a seat ornamented with a question mark, the seat of absence. The arpilleras were capable of denouncing what was happening in Chile and of revealing the innermost thoughts of the women who embroidered them. Stitching a secret pocket onto a quilt, an embroiderer placed in it a handwritten message. Often these notes spoke of a time when torture would cease and justice would prevail. One can feel the anguish of the women who so desperately want to reach others with their story. The message is both a call for hope and an act of witnessing.

On many occasions, I visited the workshops where the *arpilleristas* gathered. As they stitched, they spoke. Sometimes they needed to stop their sewing because the cloth was wet with their tears. But mutual support and love allowed them to continue embroidering the stories of their children, those they had lost, and their country. The art of the arpillera combines the individual pain of each of these women with the collective pain of all Chileans.

The arpilleristas come from many different walks of life: Pinochet's violence was indiscriminate, crushing the human rights of rich and poor. Still, while I have met professors and doctors who joined this movement, most members are from humble backgrounds—washerwomen, hotel workers, and cooks—and live in areas where there is no water or electricity.

I feel so moved by the generosity of their spirit, the solidarity that they extend to each other. I saw them feed off this spirit as they became more powerful and extended their actions to public activities, hunger strikes, and tying themselves to the gates of Congress. They became visible; they challenged fear in search of justice and assumed a central role in Chile's human rights movement. The interesting thing to note is that these women lacked any political background; they became experts through the specific experience of dealing with the disappearance of their relatives. From that moment on, the arpilleristas began to learn, eventually founding an inspiring and generous form of activism.

The art of embroidery has played a role in grassroots movements beyond Chile's borders. It had a very powerful influence in Peru, where women who had been victims of violence at the hands of the Shining Path also made arpilleras in order to tell their stories. And embroidery played an important role in Soweto, where women made quilts to denounce apartheid.

Everyone who owns an arpillera, as I do, is reminded every day of what happened in Chile, in other Latin American countries,

The message is both a call for hope and an act of witnessing.

in all of the countries where might makes right. We must always remember if we are to create a future free of hatred and violence. The arpilleristas have given us the texture of memory and truth.

Now the arpilleras are the light of Chile, the clear heart of the country. They are the legacy of dark times. They are the memory of a generation that disappeared. Nearly two decades after the end of the dictatorship, women in Santiago continue to make them, using the same appliqué techniques; their themes are often the same as those of 30 years ago. Many of today's arpilleras say NO to impunity, NO to amnesty for those who ordered and carried out the violence of the Pinochet era.

And some of their demands have been acknowledged. When Pinochet died during the summer of 2006, he did not receive the official recognition his supporters wanted. A socialist woman from the same party as Pinochet's predecessor, the former President Allende, is today the head of the government; her father was murdered under Pinochet. She leads a country that is struggling to know itself, rethinking its own identity, and daring to dream once again.

I believe that the spirit of justice and fortitude created at the birth of the arpillera movement almost 30 years ago is still very much alive in today's Chile, where a woman who was once tortured and exiled rules the country with a sense of unity and a profound belief that in order to forge a decent future Chileans must remember their grim past. The art of the arpillera is both the past and the future in my country.

This year I returned to Chile in the fall, and each golden leaf reminded me of lives cut short. I tried to gather all the leaves in my hands, and I felt that Chile was also changing seasons, entering a time of dialogues and reflections, hope and reconciliation. I felt that I could finally truly return to a country that now dares to dream—and then I realized that I no longer feared the night.

TIMELINE

1952, 1958, 1964	Socialist Senate leader Salvador Allende makes three failed attempts for the presidency under the Frente de Acción Popular (Popular Action Front).
1970	On November 3, Salvador Allende, as leader of the Unidad Popular (Popular Unity party), defeats a former president, Jorge Alessandri, to assume the presidency. Allende implements controversial social and economic reforms in his "Chilean Way to Socialism" program.
1971	Chile reestablishes political and economic ties with Cuba and Fidel Castro visits the country, lending vocal support to Allende's presidency. This act is seen by Western powers as a clear move toward communism.
1971–1972	Inflation rises precipitously in Chile, and copper, the country's chief export, loses value on the international market. The Chilean economy declines rapidly.
1973	The Christian Democrats—the majority of the Chilean Congress—and the right-wing Nationalist Party form the Confederación Democrática (Democratic Confederation) to challenge Allende's presidency.
	On June 29, Colonel Roberto Souper directs an unsuccessful coup against Allende outside the presidential palace.
	On August 22, the commander-in-chief of the Chilean army, Carlos Prats, is pressured to resign and is replaced by General Augusto Pinochet.
	The Chamber of Deputies publicly proclaims that Allende's socialist policies have violated the Chilean Constitution and led to the "breakdown" of Chilean democracy.
	On September 11, Pinochet leads the Chilean army in a violent coup that ends Allende's government and brings the country under a harsh military dictatorship. (Allende makes a farewell speech shortly before the capture of the palace and is believed to have committed suicide.)
	On September 13, Pinochet dissolves Congress. The junta (the military force that had taken over the country) establishes a detention camp for political dissidents at the National Stadium.
	On October 6, the Comité Pro-Paz (Pro-Peace Committee), a coalition of religious organizations, is organized to help people targeted by the dictatorship.

	In November, the Directorate of National Intelligence (DINA) is secretly created to eliminate, oftentimes through human rights abuses, political parties that oppose the junta.
1974	A group of women in search of disappeared family members organize the arpillera workshops.
1975	Following Pinochet's threats to abolish the Comité Pro-Paz, Cardinal Silva forms the Vicaría de la Solidaridad (Vicariate of Solidarity) to aid afflicted families and search for the disappeared.
1976	Led by newly elected President Jimmy Carter, United States legislators pass a law that restricts foreign aid to governments implicated in human rights abuses.
1978	The Chilean Supreme Court upholds a provision for amnesty for acts committed by military government officials during the first three years of the dictatorship.
1980	The military government enacts the Chilean Constitution of 1980 through a plebiscite.
1988	On October 5, under provisions in the constitution of 1980, a referendum is held to decide the country's leadership. Chileans defy Pinochet and vote for a return to democracy. The arpillera workshops under the Vicaría de la Solidaridad are dissolved. A new group of arpilleristas establishes the Fundación Solidaridad to carry on the social and political commentary of the original arpilleristas.
1989	Presidential elections are held.
1990	On March 11, Pinochet steps down and Patricio Alwyn is democratically elected president. Pinochet becomes the commander-in-chief of the army.
1991	The National Commission on Truth and Reconciliation releases the Rettig Report, which chronicles some of the human rights violations committed under the military junta.
1998	Pinochet assumes a seat in the Chilean Senate, as prescribed in the constitution of 1980.

1998	On October 16, while seeking medical treatment in London, Pinochet is arrested by British police on a warrant issued by a judge in Spain. He is charged with major human rights violations and spends more than a year under house arrest, but he is released under pressure of the Chilean government.
2000	On March 11, Ricardo Lagos, who emerged as a leader during Chile's democratic recovery of the 1980s, is elected the thirty-third president of Chile. He enjoys record approval ratings by the time his presidency expires in 2006.
	In August, the Chilean Supreme Court rescinds Pinochet's immunity. He is prosecuted but is later found unfit to stand trial on account of dementia.
2004	Sergio Valech leads an investigative commission that produces a detailed report on the human rights abuses of the Pinochet regime.
2005	In November, Pinochet is found fit to stand trial and is charged with human rights violations.
2006	On March 11, Michelle Bachelet, whose father died three decades earlier at the hands of DINA, is sworn in as Chile's first female president.
	On December 10, Augusto Pinochet dies in Santiago at the age of 91.

On September 11, 1973, a group of Chilean military officers led by General Augusto Pinochet struck down Salvador Allende's democratically elected government. Seventeen years of oppressive dictatorship followed. In a lawless state ruled by fear and the censor's pen, few had the courage to confront the system. Among them were the sisters, wives, and mothers who refused to give up on those who—for political reasons—had disappeared without a trace. In the course of their prolonged search, the women found one another. Most of them were largely marginalized, impoverished women who were forced to assume full responsibility for their families and lead them through extraordinarily difficult times. They formed workshops, taught one another practical skills, and embarked on a struggle for truth and justice. Turning to the folk art of embroidery, they found their voice: in brilliant *arpilleras* (tapestries), they told the stories of the disappeared and of other victims of the military dictatorship. With the helping hand of the Roman Catholic church, these tapestries were smuggled out of Chile and bore witness around the world to the plight of the dead and the missing.

The following essay explores several aspects of life under a dictatorship. Consider key questions:

KEY QUESTIONS

1. What could a group of impoverished women do about the disappearance of their loved ones? What kinds of tools did they use in their search for the disappeared, for a political voice, and for social change?

2. What is a dictatorship? Who holds the power and authority in a dictatorship? What democratic institutions were destroyed when Allende's regime was struck down?

3. How did the dictatorship deprive ordinary Chileans of basic rights? How can citizens in a dictatorship speak out against crimes committed by their government?

4. How can art, poetry, and storytelling call attention to social injustice and human rights violations?

The End of a Democratic Tradition

At 11:52 AM on September 11, 1973, the shriek of fighter jets pierced the sky of Chile's capital: Santiago was under attack. Two Hawker Hunter airplanes headed straight for the presidential mansion, La Moneda, and let fly their missiles. Once they had shattered La Moneda's walls and windows, tanks and foot soldiers stormed the building. Within minutes they had

Pinochet's soldiers look over the presidential palace of La Moneda during the military coup. On September 11, 1973, Pinochet ordered the military to bomb the palace and take it over.

found the body of the socialist president, Salvador Allende Gossens. The airplanes, the missiles, the tanks, the soldiers, and those who commanded them belonged not to an invading power but to the Chilean armed forces. Led by General Augusto Pinochet Ugarte, the army had put an end to the Popular Unity coalition one thousand days after it took office. It also ended 130

years of imperfect but almost uninterrupted democracy.

During the weeks and months that followed the coup,* violence spread in waves over the entire country. Formerly commander-in-chief of Allende's army, Pinochet directed a fierce and bloody war against those who remained loyal to the dead president. The military junta† that ruled Chile declared a state of siege, harshly restricting civilians' rights and expanding the authority of the military over every aspect of life. Opposition leaders were hunted down and thousands of men and women were rounded up in Santiago's National Stadium, which assumed a new role as a prison camp. There suspected opponents of the Pinochet regime were interrogated, tortured, and killed. Concentration camps were filled with people suspected of sympathies with socialism or the Popular Unity government. Residents of the capital soon grew accustomed to the sound of

---

* A coup, from the French *coup d'état*, is a swift and forceful overthrow of a government.

† The word *junta*, from a Spanish word meaning board or committee, is a group of military officers who rule a state without having been elected.

gunfire. More than three thousand people disappeared without a trace during the years of the dictatorship; the vast majority of them were executed or tortured to death without a trial. In a matter of days, Chile's fragile democracy had collapsed.

Viviana Díaz Caro, whose father was "disappeared," directed the Agrupación de Familiares de Detenidos Desaparecidos (Association of Families of the Detained-Disappeared), which collected information about the disappeared and helped their relatives fight for justice. All the *arpilleristas* belonged to this organization.[1] Caro recalls the disappearance of her father:

> Until September 11, 1973, my father was the Undersecretary of the Chilean Communist Party and Director of the National Workers (Labor) Organization. Due to the posts my father held, the armed forces and secret service agents began searching for him immediately after the coup led by General Augusto Pinochet. . . . [I]n May 1976, everything changed. They found my father in a house in the Las Condes neighborhood. . . . People who witnessed his arrest testified he was almost unconscious when they took him away. . . .
>
> The same day in the afternoon we began our desperate search. . . . At that time, we began a new phase in our lives. . . . [W]e didn't know where to go to receive information about the detained. We didn't know where they took people who were arrested. For my mother and the rest of us, it was total chaos. . . . Soon after his disappearance, we made the rounds like every other family that had detained/disappeared relatives. We began with the hospitals, jails, detention centers, the Legal

and Medical Institute, etc. The answers were always the same: this person doesn't exist, he was never arrested, and we don't have any record of this individual.[2]

Two years earlier, Violeta Morales, a poor seamstress and a leading voice among the relatives of the disappeared, had faced a similar ordeal: her brother, Newton Morales, was disappeared by Pinochet's security forces. A popular working-class leader, he was forced into hiding after resisting the coup. For a while, recalls Violeta Morales, "everything was fine." But "one morning three men and a detained woman came to my mother's house and they took Newton away."[3] The terrified family soon heard that he had been taken to Londres 38[‡], an infamous interrogation center.[4] Determined to find him and unwilling to let their fear and poverty stand in their way, the Morales family knocked on the doors of every detention center they could locate in Santiago, only to be told deliberately confusing stories about Newton's whereabouts. Despite the passionate efforts of his family, no sign of Newton Morales has ever been found. He had become one of the *desaparecidos***[**]—the haunting term applied to all those who never reappeared after they had been

---

‡ Londres 38 was one of at least a dozen torture and detention facilities in and around Santiago. Relatively small (no more than 70 detainees were there at a time), it served as a temporary prison and interrogation center.

** The term *desaparecidos* was first used by Guatemalans in the 1960s when the country's security forces engaged in a massive campaign of terror and abductions. The term is also closely associated with the thirty thousand people who disappeared during Argentina's "dirty war"—a state-sponsored terror campaign against political "subversives" that lasted from 1976 to 1983.

Arpillera 1: Created by Violeta Morales. The faceless figures next to the women represent the missing victims who dared to oppose Pinochet's dictatorship.

abducted, interrogated, and murdered by the dictatorship.

Violeta Morales turned to a church-based organization founded in Santiago by Cardinal Raúl Silva Henríquez. As soon as he learned just how brutal the Pinochet regime could be, Silva began to put together a vast interfaith effort to help political prisoners and their relatives. The result, officially announced on October 6, 1973, was the Comité de Cooperación para la Paz en Chile (Cooperative Committee for Peace in Chile), known as the Comité Pro-Paz, a group that included—in addition to Catholics—Baptists, Methodists, Lutherans, and Jews.

Religious leaders took a stand and began to document civil rights violations, especially disappearances. When Pinochet forced the Comité Pro-Paz to close its doors, Silva created the Vicaría de la Solidaridad del Arzobispado de Santiago (Vicariate of Solidarity of the Archbishop of Santiago) to carry on his humanitarian efforts. As Violeta Morales, Viviana Díaz Caro, and many other women who refused to be intimidated joined the group, it became clear that they were searching not just for their loved ones but also for a voice.

"QUESTION,"
A POEM BY DORIS MENICONI LORCA

Doris Meniconi Lorca wrote many poems for her son, Isidro Miguel Angel Pizarro, who was taken in November 1974 by the Chilean secret police. From a poor background, Isidro turned to social activism at an early age, educating and supporting peasants in their political struggle. Such work belonged to the ambitious reforms set out during Allende's presidency, when vast tracts of land were seized or purchased from the wealthy and reassigned to poor peasants. Isidro's political activism and involvement in this program earned him enemies among conservatives, the landowners he helped deprive of their property, and the dictatorship. The poem "Question" describes Doris Meniconi Lorca's torment after his disappearance.

Where is the son that I love so much?

Where is the warmth of his white hands?

When I call only silence responds.

Iron chains have left him prisoner,

and if you search blindly for your star in the night

you will only find shadows, sadness and reproaches.

What guard guards the bars of the dark cell that hides you?

They have left me a wound that is uncertainty

and I shout your name that the wind carries away,

my throat is raw from calling you.

But in your absence there is no

forgetting.

Yes, I lost the laugh that ripped the autumn.

Summers wander in my sea of bitterness,

winter goes with me with its sadness

and I let the impalpable rain kiss my forehead

asking God for the hand that wounds me with nostalgia

and I go on living from sips of the pain of knowing you are absent.

Invisible is the dagger piercing my soul

and my face carries wounds caused by weeping

the slow step of the years, and the grief beneath the song.[4]

CONNECTIONS

1. Pinochet and his supporters overthrew Allende's government by force—an act described as a coup. What democratic institutions were destroyed by the coup? What happens to a democracy when people are not free to associate, to speak out, or to show dissent? Can you give examples?

2. What could these impoverished women do against a military regime that controlled all access to power?

3. Pinochet used torture, kidnappings, and killings to terrorize his people. What was the purpose of this strategy?

4. When should religious organizations defend the voiceless and resist oppression? How should they do so? How do you think Cardinal Silva would respond to this question?

5. Thousands of people disappeared without a trace in Chile. They were called the *desaparecidos*. Lorca's poem describes the torments of a mother whose son had disappeared. How is being *disappeared* different from being arrested or detained?

6. Doris Meniconi Lorca's poem is called "Question." What question or questions does she raise? To whom are they addressed? Where can she find answers? What insights does her poem offer about life for the families of the disappeared?

---

[1] Marjorie Agosín, *Scraps of Life: Chilean Arpilleras, Chilean Women and the Pinochet Dictatorship*, trans. Cola Franzen (Toronto: Williams-Wallace Publishers, 1987), 70.

[2] Marjorie Agosín, *Tapestries of Hope, Threads of Love: The Arpillera Movement in Chile* (Lanham: Rowman & Littlefield Publishers, Inc., forthcoming).

[3] Ibid.

[4] Ibid.

The Years Before the Dictatorship

After nearly three hundred years of colonial rule, Chile won its independence from Spain in 1817. Roughly from that time until 1973, when the coup struck down Salvador Allende Gossens, the country was ruled, with few exceptions, by civilian governments. A modern constitution was approved in 1925, providing a clear basis in law for democracy. While economic and social tensions often roiled under the surface, the various groups remained committed to majority rule—class and political differences never resulted in an all-out civil war.

In 1970 the presidential incumbent, Eduardo Frei Montalva, who had held office for six years, lost the support of the middle class as he failed to cope with demands for social reforms. This opened the door to Allende's Popular Unity coalition (known as UP, the abbreviation for Unidad Popular). After a tight race, Allende, an avowed socialist, prevailed. While Allende remained committed to a peaceful transition to socialism, he also sought to deepen democracy in Chile (traditionally, this presidential democracy was heavily controlled by the business and agricultural elites). He believed that the duty of democratic societies was to ensure the well-being of all citizens and that the poor must take an active role. In a speech delivered to a rally in Santiago in the spring of 1972, Allende declared that under socialist leadership Chileans finally experienced

Used by permission of Marjorie Agosin.

Arpillera 2: Created by Violeta Morales to commemorate Salvador Allende, who instituted far-reaching policies in support of Chile's poor.

. . . a most authentic political democracy, a pluralist democracy, in government and opposition. . . . Today the people have united to defend this authentic freedom, because we have reaffirmed, expanded and deepened the individual, political, collective and social freedoms. Let this be heard and not forgotten: in this country there is not one political prisoner . . . not one journalist jailed for his ideas. . . . In this country there is a total freedom of the press and information and we have the utmost tolerance and respect for all creeds.

These liberties are greater than ever in the history of Chile. . . . But these liberties, though fundamental, are not sufficient. We also want economic freedom for Chile and each Chilean. . . . Chileans will be truly free when we are rid of ignorance, unemployment, exploitation, hunger and moral and physiological misery.[1]

Supporters of Allende's socialist ideas of democracy, which involved a redistribution of wealth and ensured liberties such as freedom of the press, line the street.

Despite the incessant hostility of opposition newspapers, Allende saw to it that their freedom of speech was never threatened during his time in office.[2] He also confronted large disparities in income because, he argued, poverty undermined basic democratic values and inhibited creativity.[3] In a speech given on the first anniversary of his inauguration, Allende reflected on his party's democratic vision:

> That is why we have been gaining power; we have been incorporating deprived groups and sectors. We have been concerned with strengthening democracy and expanding liberties through the redistribution of income and economic liberation.
>
> This government wants an authentic democracy and complete freedom for all Chileans. Democracy and freedom are incompatible with unemployment and lack of housing, the lack of culture, illiteracy and sickness. How is democracy strengthened? By creating more jobs, giving better wages, building more homes, providing the people with more culture, education and better health.[4]

To address these issues, Allende drew up ambitious plans. These included nationalizing mines and industries, donating expropriated* land to poor agrarian laborers, mandating low prices for food staples, and increasing the minimum wage. Other measures were taken to ensure better housing and education for the poor.

Students, middle-class professionals, factory workers, and peasants had come together in support of a candidate who had for many years been deemed unelectable. Many believed they had witnessed the birth of a new form of Chilean politics. For poor women such as Violeta Morales and Viviana Díaz Caro, Allende came to represent the possibility of sustained employment, decent housing, and public

---

* *Expropriation* is the act of seizing privately owned property and giving it to others. Typically this means taking land from the rich and giving it to the poor. The process is often forceful, though the original owners may be paid for their lost property. During his rule, Allende attempted to expropriate lands held for generations by the agrarian elite (though the process was never completed); he also seized parts of Chile's rich mines, which largely benefited foreign companies.

healthcare services for children and adults. One Chilean wrote, "People believed that paradise was around the corner. There was an explosion of passion, a drunken binge of ideas."[5] Around the world, progressive groups watched with excitement as Allende's *via Chilena*—a peaceful and democratic revolution—unfolded.

Despite high expectations and plenty of revolutionary rhetoric, the mood of the country soon soured and pressure from both left and right threatened the new programs. Allende's supporters demanded that he accelerate the pace of social reforms, while these same plans provoked protests from conservatives, including big landowners, large and small business owners, and the military.[†] Despite promises of peaceful reforms, many feared a Soviet-style communism, with a tyrannical government trampling on human rights and private property. The opposition's newspapers and radio stations spread rumors of armed revolution, calling on volunteers to arm themselves and patrol wealthy neighborhoods. Adding to this growing sense of crisis were empty grocery store shelves, violent strikes, and skyrocketing prices. By the middle of 1973 the national economy was in shambles.

Mired in Cold War politics, the administration of United States President Richard Nixon anxiously followed the events unfolding in Santiago. American politicians feared that a socialist government would tip the balance of power in Latin America, giving the Soviet Union a clear advantage—they decided the time had come to undermine Allende's presidency.[6] In 1975 the United States Senate appointed a committee to investigate the United States' involvement in Chile. Although it found no evidence that the CIA was directly involved in the coup that overthrew Allende, the committee concluded that the United States sponsored anti-Allende propaganda, backed his political rivals, promoted plots to overthrow the government, and suspended almost all foreign aid to the struggling regime.[7]

In response to mounting chaos, Chilean right-wing organizations, which played a major role in the destruction of the civil order, demanded that the army intervene to restore order. Suburban right-wing women who opposed Allende organized the dramatic "March of the Empty Pots," parading through Santiago while banging their empty cooking pots to protest food shortages. These women, later among Pinochet's most outspoken champions, taunted the soldiers sent to police the march, threw corn at them while calling them chickens, and prodded them to take over the government.[8] In spite of elections held in March 1973 that showed unmistakable support for Allende's programs, high-ranking military officers decided that Chile was ripe for a military takeover. On September 11, 1973, they acted.

[†] During Allende's presidency, impatient laborers took matters into their own hands and seized agrarian property. In towns, workers organized and took over several factories. For more information about factory takeovers and the tension between Allende and his left-wing supporters, see Peter Winn, *Weavers of Revolution: The Yarur Workers and Chile's Road to Socialism* (New York: Oxford University Press, 1986).

"ESTADIO CHILE," VICTOR JARA'S LAST POEM, SEPTEMBER 1973

Victor Jara was born in a small, rural town outside Santiago. His family was poor and belonged to the many that fought for Allende's election in the hope for vast economic reforms. Jara, who became one of Chile's most beloved folk artists, devoted his music to industrial workers, peasants, and the poor residents of Chile's shantytowns (many of the arpilleristas came from these overcrowded neighborhoods). His lyrics carried a message of hope to ordinary Chileans and attempted to capture their daily hardships and political aspirations. When Allende was elected, Jara became a devoted supporter of the new regime. Shortly after the coup, Jara was arrested and was taken to the Stadium of Chile (hence the name of the following song), where he was tortured and killed. Prisoners at the stadium reported that Jara scribbled this last poem on a piece of paper just before his death and that a friend smuggled it out. The poem, which was later translated into English by Joan Jara, Victor's wife, describes and comments on the conditions in the stadium in the days following the coup. The stadium is now called Estadio Victor Jara.

> There are five thousand of us here
> in this small part of the city.
> We are five thousand.
> I wonder how many we are in all
> in the cities and in the whole country?
> Here alone
> are ten thousand hands which plant seeds
> and make the factories run.
> How much humanity
> exposed to hunger, cold, panic, pain,
> moral pressure, terror and insanity?
> Six of us were lost
> as if into starry space.
> One dead, another beaten as I could never have believed
> a human being could be beaten.
> The other four wanted to end their terror—
> one jumping into nothingness,
> another beating his head against a wall,
> but all with the fixed stare of death.
> What horror the face of fascism creates!
> They carry out their plans with knife-like precision.
> Nothing matters to them.
> To them, blood equals medals,
> slaughter is an act of heroism.
> Oh God, is this the world that you created,

for this your seven days of wonder and work?
Within these four walls only a number exists
which does not progress,
which slowly will wish more and more for death.
But suddenly my conscience awakes
and I see that this tide has no heartbeat,
only the pulse of machines
and the military showing their midwives' faces
full of sweetness.
Let Mexico, Cuba and the world
cry out against this atrocity!
We are ten thousand hands
which can produce nothing.
How many of us in the whole country?
The blood of our president, our compañero,
will strike with more strength than bombs and machine guns!
So will our fist strike again!

How hard it is to sing
when I must sing of horror.
Horror which I am living,
horror which I am dying.
To see myself among so much
and so many moments of infinity
in which silence and screams
are the end of my song.
What I see, I have never seen
What I have felt and what I feel
Will give birth to the moment . . . .[9]

CONNECTIONS

1. What did Allende's party stand for? How important is freedom of speech for democracy? How important is freedom from persecution and fear?

2. How did Allende seek to deepen democracy in Chile? What economic conditions did he consider necessary for a just and vibrant democracy? Why did his plans fail? How could they have succeeded?

3. Why did Chile's conservative elites oppose Allende's plans for Chile? What did they fear?

4. Under pressure from the political right and left, Allende's regime collapsed into chaos and violence. What are the legitimate ways to express disagreement and dissent in a democratic regime?

5. Victor Jara's poem begins with taking count of the people imprisoned in the stadium after the coup:

    There are five thousand of us here

    in this small part of the city.

    We are five thousand.

    I wonder how many we are in all

    in the cities and in the whole country?

    Who is the "we" that Jara is describing?

6. What words and phrases does Jara use to describe the abuses of the dictatorship? What does he suggest was lost?

7. Jara uses the word *fascism* to describe the dictatorship. What does the term mean? What other regimes were called fascist?

[1] Salvador Allende, "Here Are Assembled the People of Chile (1972)," quoted in *Salvador Allende Reader: Chile's Voice of Democracy*, ed. James D. Cockroft, trans. Moisés Espinoza and Nancy Nuñez (New York: Ocean Press, 2000), 149–50.

[2] Lisa Baldez, *Why Women Protest: Women's Movements in Chile* (Cambridge: Cambridge University Press, 2002), 102–3.

[3] Allende, "Here Are Assembled the People of Chile," *Salvador Allende Reader*, 149–50.

[4] Salvador Allende, "First Anniversary of the Popular Government (November 4, 1971)," *Salvador Allende Reader*, 119–20.

[5] Pamela Constable and Arturo Valenzuela, *A Nation of Enemies: Chile Under Pinochet* (New York: Norton, 1991), 25.

[6] Peter Kornbluh, *The Pinochet File: A Declassified Dossier on Atrocity and Accountability* (New York: New Press, 2003), 79–152. This book documents the United States' involvement in Chile's politics during the regimes of Allende and Pinochet.

[7] The committee was headed by Senator Frank Church (a Democratic senator from Idaho). See "Church Report: Covert Action in Chile 1963–1973," United States Department of State website, http://foia.state.gov/Reports/ChurchReport.asp#A.%20Overview:%20Cover%20Action%20in%20Chile (accessed February 13, 2007).

[8] Baldez, *Why Women Protest*, 81. The opposition claimed the march showed that Allende's regime had lost its legitimacy (particularly among women). Allende's supporters claimed that the march had been organized by right-wing extremists and insisted that the rich women who joined the march had never known a moment's hunger and certainly had never cooked in the pots they clanged.

[9] Victor Jara, "Estadio Chile," quoted in Joan Jara, *An Unfinished Song: The Life of Victor Jara* (New York: Ticknor & Fields, 1984), 250–51.

The Dictatorship and the Disappeared

The coup was violent, swift, and successful. Within a few hours Chile's democratic dream disappeared. Over the next 17 years, Chileans knew little or no political freedom. The military junta answered to no one. After the hope, frustration, and lively debates of the Allende period, this was a time of violence, corruption, lack of accountability, and arbitrary rule. Patricia Hidalgo, one of those who eventually stood up and protested the regime's brutality, presents her experience of the change:

> In the beginning, when there was the coup, I didn't understand the importance of what had happened. But, when the military came to our communities, to the shantytowns, they grabbed the men and beat them. That is when I understood the repercussions of the coup. . . . We were so afraid because in the morning, when we woke up, everything was blocked off and I wondered, what kind of life is this? Men without work, one person sustaining everything and in fear. Everyone was very suspicious of everyone else and we felt we couldn't talk to anyone because we had no idea who they might be talking to.[1]

Barricades, massive unemployment, terror—civil life (what sociologists often call *civil society*) had collapsed. Repression replaced the most valuable things in a free regime—the institutions and practices that guarantee citizens the right to conduct their economic, social, and political affairs without fear of government retaliation. Elections, representative bodies, free speech, and the right to protest vanished, and the dictatorship launched an all-

Used by permission of Marjorie Agosín.

Arpillera 3: A woman and man are blindfolded and chained up in the National Stadium while soldiers aim guns at them. This arpillera depicts and protests the brutality of Pinochet's dictatorship.

out war against anybody who looked threatening. It sealed all media outlets, suspended all political parties, and destroyed any group that dissented. Viviana Díaz Caro says, "It was difficult for people who hadn't lived our reality to understand the conditions Chileans lived in back then." During most of the years of the dictatorship, people "couldn't even go to the press," she continued,

> because there hadn't been freedom of the press for many years. The newspapers, TV channels, and radio were controlled. . . . The only news published was that approved by the government; even the publishing houses only printed books that were passed by the dictatorship's censors. An attorney, who defended one of the petitions in July 1976 for the protection of our father, Mr. Eugenio

Velasco, was expelled from the country a month later. Justice disappeared when the dictatorship took control, because not only was crime punished, ideas were too.[2]

The new regime closely observed leftist organizations and arrested many of their members. When a few members of the Movimiento de Izquierda Revolucionaria (Movement of the Revolutionary Left, known as the MIR) took arms in an improvised act of resistance to the dictatorship, everybody suspected of connection with the organization was hunted down. Devorah Gotthelf* was a young student and an activist when the military junta struck down Allende's government. She was also a member of the MIR and among the first to be disappeared and cruelly tortured by the junta's secret services. Gotthelf argued that the idealist members of this organization objected to what they called the "imperialist" interference of the Soviet Union and the United States in South America. In addition, members of the organization worked for years to improve the lot of Chile's laboring poor. It was, she recalled, "a very intellectual and theoretical [organization]," in which members shared a romantic dream of participating in "'armed struggle'... but [they] had no real 'armed' training, no arms, and no infrastructure to support this practice."[3]

In 1970, when Allende campaigned for the presidential election, the MIR gave up its militant, revolutionary aspirations and joined his coalition. After the coup,

the organization's enthusiastic support of Allende's reforms made it a prime target for the junta and "most of the MIR activists were imprisoned, assassinated, or disappeared."[4] The group that carried out the systematic persecution of MIR activists was the Dirección de Inteligencia Nacional (National Intelligence Directorate, called the DINA), Pinochet's secret police.[†] Created shortly after the coup and led by a notorious general named Manuel Contreras, the organization carried out its mandate to collect intelligence about subversives by abducting, torturing, and murdering thousands of men and women. Violeta Morales, whose brother Newton was sought because of his association with MIR, describes the secret police's methods:

> The first time they came looking for my brother, my mother was alone. The men asked for Newton and told her they were friends from work. They returned that evening at 9:00. Nobody was home yet. . . . The men passed themselves off as co-workers and my mother believed them. When Newton came home the men took him by the arms and he called out to my mother, who was in the kitchen, "Mother, the DINA is taking me away." My mother didn't understand what was happening at the time because she had never been political. The men tried to [calm] her because she was grasping my brother. One of the agents took

*A pseudonym is used to protect this witness's identity.

† Pinochet shrewdly turned MIR's militant reputation against the group. He announced to the media that communists, Cubans, and MIR had drawn up a plot he called Plan Z, which the military junta was able to avert only by staging its own coup on September 11. We now know that Plan Z was a fiction jointly created by Chilean military intelligence and the CIA. On the CIA's involvement, see "Hinchey Report" (2000), United States Department of State website, http://foia.state.gov/Reports/HincheyReport.asp#toc (accessed February 13, 2007).

Thousands of people were detained, tortured, and even executed in the National Stadium during the first days of the coup.

© Bettmann/Corbis

her aside and said, "Don't worry ma'am; we'll bring him back in ten minutes—we only want to speak with him. We're friends from work."[5]

When his family traced him later, Newton Morales's trail led as far as the front gates of Londres 38: he had become one of the disappeared.

To justify the persecution of members of the MIR and many other enemies of the junta, the government spread false rumors about communist conspiracies. The DINA and other secret organizations persecuted everyone suspected of ties to the Communist Party or Allende's government. According to recently declassified CIA reports and the independent research of human rights organizations, more than 7,000 people were jailed at the National Stadium in the first days after the coup; it is estimated that 6,500 others were detained and tortured in other facilities.[6] Many of these political prisoners were summarily executed.

In the months that followed the coup, some 4,000 others were detained every month under conditions that grossly violated the constitution; hasty executions were common. "Within six months [the military] had arrested 80,000 persons, and 160,000 suffered politically motivated job dismissals. An estimated 200,000 persons, including political refugees and their family members, went into exile."[7] More than 3,000 people were murdered in Chile for political reasons between 1973 and 1990.[8] Many of Latin America's twentieth-century dictators adopted identical practices: the regional total is 90,000 *desaparecidos*.[‡]

Poet and human rights activist Marjorie Agosín describes the somber mood in the streets of Chile's capital. A hush fell over the crowded neighborhoods of Santiago, "a phantasmagorical atmosphere" broken only by the sound of police sirens and gunshots,

---

‡ Many Latin American states were ruled by military dictatorships during the 1970s and 1980s. Many carried out brutal campaigns against their political enemies.

prompting a deep "sense of stillness and desolation." The "plazas were empty," she continued,

> the courtyards without the laughter of children. Fear was in the air; you could feel the night and the police cars patrolling the cities that no longer belonged to the people. . . . Chilean society slowly began to sink into fear and silence. Every conversation with a stranger was potentially suspicious, and if one denounced the ruling government, it could have been fatal. Every cab driver was possibly a spy for the feared secret police.

> The city seemed abandoned, stripped of the noises and gestures of life. . . .

> I remember the most impressive, yet painful, aspect of the early years of the military dictatorship was a sense of void, a still and defeated silence that expunged from us the possibility of life and laughter.[9]

Neighbors turned against each other; families fell apart. Idle gossip with a neighbor could lead to betrayal, arrest, even death. "We gradually became a nation of strangers," Agosín recalls.[10]

"CHILEAN EXECUTIONS," DEPARTMENT OF STATE BRIEFING MEMORANDUM, NOVEMBER 23, 1973

A few weeks after the coup, the CIA station in Santiago sent a secret memorandum to the American secretary of state, Henry Kissinger. Based on information obtained directly from the junta, the memorandum provided the earliest reliable data about the number of people arrested and executed during the first weeks of the dictatorship.

The memorandum focused on summary executions (the killing of citizens without a trial) and executions that resulted from "court martial sentences" (sentences handed down by military courts). It suggested that the military junta was waging an all-out war against those who opposed it and that thousands of Allende's supporters had been rounded up and interrogated in the National Stadium; hundreds were known to have been killed. The junta, according to the report, claimed that a "state of siege" and martial law justified on-the-spot execution in cases of suspected "treason, armed resistance, illegal possession of arms," and even "auto theft."

The regime attempted to give its action an air of legitimacy by reigning in and organizing its intelligence services. It also postponed the military trials of leftist politicians. These actions, however, did not stop the abduction and shooting of civilians.

DEPARTMENT OF STATE BRIEFING MEMORANDUM

SECRET–NODIS

TO: The Secretary [of State, Henry Kissinger]

FROM: ARA — Jack B. Kubisch

Chilean Executions

You requested by cable from Tokyo a report on this subject.

On October 24 the Junta announced that summary, on-the-spot executions would no longer be carried out and that persons caught in the act of resisting the government would henceforth be held for military courts. Since that date 17 executions following military trials have been announced. Publicly acknowledged executions, both summary and in compliance with court martial sentences, now total approximately 100, with an additional 40 prisoners shot while "trying to escape." An internal, confidential report prepared for the Junta puts the number of executions for the period September 11–30 at 320. The latter figure is probably a more accurate indication of the extent of this practice.

Our best estimate is that the military and police units in the field are generally complying with the order to desist from summary executions. At least the rather frequent use of random violence that marked the operations of these units in the early post-coup days has clearly abated for the time being. However, there are no indications as yet of a disposition to forego executions after military trial.

The Chilean leaders justify these executions as entirely legal in the application of martial law under what they have declared to be a "state of siege in time of war." Their code of military justice permits death by firing squad for a range of offenses, including treason, armed resistance, illegal possession of arms, and auto theft. Sentences handed down by military tribunals during a state of siege are not reviewable by civilian courts.

The purpose of the executions is in part to discourage by example those who seek to organize armed opposition to the Junta. The Chilean military, persuaded to some degree by years of Communist Party propaganda, expected to be confronted by heavy resistance when they overthrew Allende. Fear of civil war was an important factor in their decision to employ a heavy hand from the outset. Also present is a puritanical, crusading spirit—a determination to cleanse and rejuvenate Chile. (A number of those executed seem to have been petty criminals.)

The Junta now has more confidence in the security situation and more awareness of the pressure of international opinion. It may be a hopeful sign that the Junta continues to stall on bringing to trial former cabinet ministers and other prominent Marxists—people the military initially had every intention of standing up before firing squads. How the military leaders proceed in this area from now on will be influenced to some degree by outside opinion, and particularly by ours, but the major consideration will continue to be their assessment of the security situation.

SECRET

Situation Report: Chile

The country is calm at the moment and there is little overt challenge to the military's firm control. Seven leftists reportedly died in an attack earlier this week on a military post in a Southern city. This, however, was the first such leftist initiative since mid-September. The general impression is that the Marxist left has given first priority to underground survival in the face of unrelenting pressure.

The Junta has announced that state-of-siege measures will remain in force for at least another eight months, but they have relaxed the curfew somewhat, revoked on-the-spot executions, placed some restrictions on searches, and promised that persons charged with civil offenses committed before the coup will be prosecuted under standard civil procedures. Although the traditional parties are well represented on the commission charged with drafting a new constitution, there is growing apprehension among them that the Junta's "anti-political" orientation will close off normal political activity for a long time to come. Again ruling out any timetable for turning Chile back to the civilians, Junta President Pinochet reinforced these fears by placing much of the blame for the country's present state on politicians in general.[11]

CONNECTIONS

1. The memorandum records the actions taken by the dictatorship against Chilean civilians. What civil rights did the Pinochet regime violate? What institutions crumbled? What democratic principles do dictators violate? In terms of individual rights and public institutions, what are the main differences between democratic and dictatorial regimes?

2. The authors of the CIA report claimed that the "Junta now has more . . . awareness of the pressure of international opinion." In what ways did public opinion modify the junta's actions? Can you think of other events in which public opinion mattered? When it did not? When should the international community move from the expression of outrage to political and even military intervention?

3. Maurice Ogden's "The Hangman" (for the text go to www.propertyrightsresearch. org/articles6/hangman_by_maurice_o.htm) presents civic complacency as the seedbed for cruel, tyrannical regimes. In the poem, a mysterious hangman comes to town and erects a gallows for his victims. When asked who these victims would be, the hangman presents the townspeople with a riddle:

   > Then a twinkle grew in his buckshot eye
   > and he gave a riddle instead of reply.
   > "He who serves me best," said he
   > "Shall earn the rope on the gallows-tree."

   Read the whole poem. What is the solution to the hangman's riddle? What do you think Ogden is trying to say about human behavior under tyranny? In what ways does the poem speak to the rise of Pinochet's government?

4. "The Hangman" presents a bleak, almost surreal picture of life under a bloodthirsty tyrant. Marjorie Agosín calls up similar images, describing the sense of void and stillness in Chile right after the coup (see page 16). In her words, the empty plazas, the absence of children's laughter, and the fear of strangers symbolize the destruction of democracy. Compare the imagery in the two texts. What do the two descriptions have in common? Think of the empty plazas, the absence of children, and the silence of the crowd in the two texts. What do they have to do with democracy? How do the two authors explain the breakdown of civic life?

BEYOND THE READING

For an animated version of Maurice Ogden's poem, see Les Goldman and Paul Julian, *The Hangman*, VHS (Carlsbad: CRM McGraw-Hill Films, 1964). The tape is available at the Facing History and Ourselves Resource Library.

[1] Marjorie Agosín, *Tapestries of Hope, Threads of Love: The Arpillera Movement in Chile* (Lanham: Rowman & Littlefield Publishers, Inc., forthcoming).

[2] Ibid.

[3] Devorah Gotthelf, personal communication with the author, May 24, 2007.

[4] Ibid.

[5] Agosín, *Tapestries of Hope, Threads of Love.*

[6] Peter Kornbluh, *The Pinochet File: A Declassified Dossier on Atrocity and Accountability* (New York: New Press, 2003), 153–54.

[7] Kenneth M. Roberts, *Deepening Democracy? The Modern Left and Social Movements in Chile and Peru* (Stanford: Stanford University Press), 95.

[8] "The Inescapable Obligation of the International Community to Bring to Justice Those Responsible for Crimes Against Humanity Committed During the Military Government in Chile," *Amnesty International*, October 29, 1998, http://web.amnesty.org/library/Index/engAMR220161998 (accessed November 14, 2005). See also John Dinges, *The Condor Years: How Pinochet and His Allies Brought Terrorism to Three Continents* (New York: New Press, 2004), 67. Dinges documents the collaboration of six Latin American dictatorships to spy on, intimidate, and kill their opponents around the world. It is estimated that 30,000 Argentinians were disappeared during the violent suppression of imaginary and real enemies in what was called the dirty war.

[9] Agosín, *Tapestries of Hope, Threads of Love.*

[10] Ibid.

[11] Department of State, "Chilean Executions," November 16, 1973, *Chile and United States: Declassified Documents Relating to the Military Coup*, 1970–1976, George Washington University website, www.gwu.edu/~nsarchiv/NSAEBB/NSAEBB8/ch10-01.htm (accessed March 22, 2007).

Taking a Stand Against Pinochet: The Catholic Church and the Disappeared

In Pinochet's Chile, Roman Catholic priests played a central role in defending the rights of the poor and the disenfranchised. Early in her search for her brother, Violeta Morales found the church her only support:

> After our brother's disappearance, we began looking for him everywhere—like all the relatives of the detained. . . . We began doing things immediately and found out that at the Pro-Paz Committee, which was located on Santa Monica Street, they were getting all types of reports about abuses and violations of human rights. We began looking for our brother in jails, cemeteries, morgues, commissaries, and anywhere a military regiment existed. We also went to the law courts, and at many of the places we went, they received us with machine guns just for asking questions and for going around searching for the detained-disappeared. We sent thousands of letters abroad asking for help as well. We even went so far as sending letters to the leaders of the dictatorship themselves, but nothing came of all this.[1]

The man behind the interfaith Comité Pro-Paz was Cardinal Raúl Silva Henríquez. Shortly after the coup, Silva, who had served as archbishop of Santiago since the 1960s, stepped into the role of "upstander," a term the author and activist Samantha Power coined to distinguish people who stand up to injustice—often at great personal risk—from "bystanders."

The clampdown on newspapers, radio and television stations, and political parties left the church the sole remaining public voice. Soon after the coup, Silva and other church leaders published a declaration condemning and expressing sorrow for the

Cardinal Raúl Silva Henríquez (center) was instrumental in speaking out against General Pinochet (right of Silva) and his abuse of human rights. Cardinal Silva established the Comité Pro-Paz to help families of the disappeared.

bloodshed. This was a fundamental turning point for many members of the Chilean clergy: some of them, including Cardinal Silva, had previously believed that only a military intervention could restore law and order. The cardinal visited the National Stadium and, shocked by the scale of the government crackdown, instructed his aides to begin collecting information from the thousands flocking to the church for refuge. Silva's actions led to an open conflict with Pinochet, who did not hesitate to threaten the church and the Comité Pro-Paz.

Undeterred, the organization soon "had established a large network in order to help relatives of the disappeared and had provided information to the press and international organizations regarding human rights abuses in Chile. . . . By mid-1974 [it] had 103 staff members in Santiago and 95 others in the provinces."[2] The work of the Comité Pro-Paz helped Violeta Morales realize that she was not alone in her search. She tells us that

> At the Pro-Paz Committee we realized that every day more people were arriving with problems like ours. After getting together with all these people, we decided to form a coordinating committee to get better organized. Without naming the people involved, we took turns directing the organization so that everyone would have a chance to learn and gain experience looking for help in our cause. Father Daniel, a French priest who was expelled from Chile and [exiled to] Peru, together with a nun called Maria de los Angeles, were the first ones to welcome us into the Pro-Paz Committee. They received us and gave us support and comfort in the first hours of desperation and grief.[3]

All together, the Comité Pro-Paz established 24 offices, all of them working under constant threats and routine harassment by the authorities. At the end of 1975, Pinochet announced that the dissident group had been banned once and for all.

In response, Cardinal Silva founded Vicaría de la Solidaridad on January 1, 1976, to carry on the work of the Comité Pro-Paz. As part of the archdiocese, the new group was protected under the country's religious laws: the church was recognized as an independent political entity and a sanctuary. The vicariate managed to continue its work until the end of the dictatorship.

Many who sought the assistance of the

Used by permission of Marjorie Agosín.

Arpillera 4: After the disappearance of their husbands, fathers, brothers, and sons, women often gathered at soup kitchens organized by the church where they sought comfort and moral support.

new organization had suffered a double blow: deprived of a family member, they themselves were often targeted because of their political beliefs. Author Isabel Allende, niece of the slain president, explains:

> Poor women in the shantytowns were the main victims of the new regime. Thousands of them became the only providers for their homes, as their husbands, fathers, and sons disappeared or roamed the country looking for menial jobs. Repression destroyed their families, extreme poverty paralyzed them, and fear condemned them to silence.[4]

As they struggled along, these women ceased to think and act as victims and became politically active. As Violeta Morales explains, this was a profound change: "We were used to the fact that here in Chile it was the men who got involved in politics, while we women dedicated ourselves to our homes and to our children, nothing more."[5] Under the church's protection they began to heal their wounded families even as they took jobs outside the home for the first time. And they found their voice.

"CHILE UNDER THE GUN," AN EXCERPT FROM *MY INVENTED COUNTRY* BY ISABEL ALLENDE

In her book, *My Invented Country: A Nostalgic Journey Through Chile*, the author, playwright, and novelist Isabel Allende (niece of Salvador Allende) discusses the painful issue of Chileans' failure to stand up to the everyday crimes of the dictatorship. Without discounting the challenges Allende's presidency faced, Isabel Allende explores the enduring weakness of democratic culture in Chile. "The hard question," she claims, "is why at least one third of Chile's total population backed the dictatorship." She suggests that a large segment of society approved of the actions taken by the dictatorial regime and was quite ready to trade civil liberties for a certain kind of order and stability. She also says that while fear of repression led some to support the harsh dictator, the totalitarian regime spoke to a wider authoritarian tendency within society fundamentally at odds with democracy.

In Chile, where friendship and family are very important, something happened that can be explained only by the effect that fear has on the soul of a society. Betrayal and denunciation snuffed out many lives; all it took was an anonymous voice over the telephone for the badly named intelligence services to sink their claws into the accused, and, in many cases, nothing was ever heard of that person again. People were divided between those who backed the military government and those who opposed it; hatred, distrust, and fear poisoned relationships. Democracy was restored more than a decade ago, but that division can still be felt, even in the heart of many families. . . .

The hard question is why at least one third of Chile's total population backed the dictatorship, even though, for most, life wasn't easy, and even adherents of the military government lived in fear. Repression was far-reaching, although there's no doubt that the poor and the leftists suffered most. Everyone felt he was being spied on, no one could say that he was completely safe from the claws of the state. It is a fact that information was censored and brainwashing was the goal of a vigorous propaganda machine; it is also true that the opposition lost many years and a lot of blood before it could get organized. But none of this explains the dictator's popularity. The percentage of the population that approved of him was not motivated solely by fear: Chileans like authority. They believed that the military was going to "clean up" the country. "They put an end to delinquency, we don't see walls defaced with graffiti any more, everything is clean, and, thanks to the curfew, our husbands get home early," one friend told me. For her, those things compensated for the loss of civil rights because she wasn't directly affected: she was in the fortunate position of not having her children lose their jobs without compensation, or of being arrested. I understand why the economic right, which, historically, has not been characterized as a defender of democracy, and which, during those years, made more money than ever before, backed the dictatorship, but what about the rest? I haven't found a satisfactory answer to that question, only conjectures.

Pinochet represented the intransigent father, capable of imposing strict discipline. The three years of the Unidad Popular were a time of experimentation, change, and disorder; the country was weary. Repression put an end to politicking, and neoliberalism forced Chileans to work, keep their mouths closed, and be productive, so that corporations could compete favorably in international markets. Nearly everything was privatized, including health, education, and social security. The need to survive drove private initiative. . . .

Who was Pinochet, really? . . . Why was he so feared? Why was he admired? I never met him personally, and I didn't live in Chile during the greater part of his government, so I can only judge him by his actions and what others have written about him. I suppose that, to understand Pinochet, you need to read novels such as Mario Vargas Llosa's *Feast of the Goat* or Gabriel Garcia Marquez's *Autumn of the Patriarch*, because he had a lot in common with the typical figure of the Latin American *caudillo* (leader) so aptly described by those authors. He was a crude, cold, slippery, authoritarian man who had no scruples or sense of loyalty other than to the army as an institution—though not to his comrades in arms, whom he had killed according to his convenience, men such as General Carlos Prats and others. He believed that he was chosen by God and history to save his country. . . . He was astute and suspicious, but he could be genial, and, at times, even likeable. Admired by some, despised by others, feared by all, he was possibly the man in our history who has held the greatest power in his hands for the longest period of time. . . .

The military coup didn't come out of nowhere; the forces that upheld the dictatorship were there, we just hadn't perceived them. Defects that had lain there beneath the surface blossomed in all their glory and majesty during that period. It isn't possible that repression on such a grand scale could have been organized overnight unless a totalitarian tendency already existed in a sector of the society; apparently, we were not as democratic as we believed. As for the government of Salvador Allende, it wasn't as innocent as I like to imagine; it suffered from ineptitude, corruption, and pride. In real life, it may not always be easy to distinguish between heroes and villains, but I can assure you that in democratic governments, including that of the Unidad Popular, there was never the cruelty the nation has suffered every time the military intervenes.[6]

CONNECTIONS

1. Where can victims of a repressive society find solace, support, and venues to express their outrage? How can they speak when their governments work to silence all criticism?

2. What qualities and authority do religious leaders like Cardinal Silva bring to the struggle against abusive regimes? What advantages might they have had that others did not?

3. Cardinal Silva was an "upstander." Why do some people and institutions speak out against injustice while others remain silent?

4. In her pioneering work, *Accounting for Genocide* (Free Press, 1979), sociologist Helen Fein defines the circle of people to whom we owe some sort of debt as our "universe of obligation." What was Cardinal Silva's universe of obligation after the coup? What is your universe of obligation?

5. In the essay, Isabel Allende explains that a large segment of the Chilean population chose to be bystanders to the actions of the dictatorship; many, she argues, even welcomed it. According to Allende, what reasons motivated supporters of the dictatorship? Why do you think some people and institutions support regimes that violate human rights?

---

[1] Marjorie Agosín, *Tapestries of Hope, Threads of Love: The Arpillera Movement in Chile* (Lanham: Rowman & Littlefield Publishers, Inc., forthcoming).

[2] Mario I. Aguilar, "Cardinal Raúl Silva Henríquez, The Catholic Church, and the Pinochet Regime, 1973–1980: Public Responses to a National Security State," *The Catholic Historical Review* 8, no. 4 (October 2003), 724.

[3] Agosín, *Tapestries of Hope, Threads of Love.*

[4] Isabel Allende, "Foreword," *Tapestries of Hope, Threads of Love.*

[5] Agosín, *Tapestries of Hope, Threads of Love.*

[6] Isabel Allende, *My Invented Country: A Nostalgic Journey Through Chile* (New York: HarperCollins Publishers, Inc., 2003) 160–71.

Arpillera 1
Women and the disappeared

Arpillera 2
Chileans show support for Salvador Allende

Arpillera 3
Prisoners in the National Stadium

Arpillera 4
Families of the disappeared at a church-sponsored soup kitchen

Arpillera 5
Arpillera workshop in a church basement

Arpillera 6
Women dancing alone ("La Cueca Sola")

Arpillera 7
Women organizing a nonviolent protest

Arpillera 8
Rebuilding democracy

STITCHING TRUTH

Finding a Voice in Solidarity and Art

The distraught women who came to the Vicaría de la Solidaridad created a number of cooperative enterprises—soup kitchens, laundries, educational workshops—as well as the *arpillera* workshops. These women were desperately poor: about 80 percent of them had no money and no obvious prospect for any. But "from despair," says Violeta Morales, "emerged the idea of making arpilleras." For lack of material, "we got the idea of cutting up our clothes and unraveling our sweaters to make the first arpilleras."[1] Soon they began to stitch together pieces of old cloth they had collected, using the domestic skills of embroidery, sewing, and knitting to make something they could sell. They then struck a deal with the church: in return for their tapestries, the vicariate would pay a small fee. The income from transactions saved hundreds of Santiago families.

Valentina Bonne, an artist who taught many of the arpilleristas how to sew, weave, and embroider, says that when the workshops first opened the women were still so shattered that they had to use this art form as a kind of therapy. Violeta Morales recalls her early experience in the arpillera workshop:

> We opened our workshop in 1974, but we didn't go public until 1975. In those years, I took on full responsibility for the search of my brother. My sister had been kidnapped by a cab driver who interrogated her about the names of people she knew. . . . After that my sister was afraid to go out into the street to look for our brother. I was scared too. We were all afraid to keep on asking and searching. Then I put all my energy into the arpillera workshop; it was sometimes the only thing that kept me balanced emotionally. There I found other people who were suffering from the same thing and trying to help them sometimes helped me with my own tragedy.[2]

These tapestries are a folk art with a long tradition. The Chilean folksinger Violeta Parra was a famed arpillerista who created lively, politically themed arpilleras in the 1960s. "She spoke for the poor and the oppressed," wrote Agosín,

Women come together to support each other and study the pictures of missing family members. More than 3,000 people disappeared and were executed during Pinochet's dictatorship.

© Diego Goldberg/Sygma/Corbis.

"and became a symbol, especially for the young and the compassionate part of the population, and was an inspiration for artists of all persuasions."[3] This symbolism of the arpilleras made in Pinochet's Chile made them unique. From the very beginning, Morales argued,

> We wanted to do something different. We didn't want to make something that would function as a decoration. We wanted to design a handmade product that would denounce what we and our country were living through. . . . We wanted to embroider our story, the harsh and sad story of our ruined country.[4]

The first arpilleras made at the vicariate were assembled hastily. Simple stitches, rough and colorful cloth, and basic embroidery conveyed the fragmented experience of the women who made them. They were fragile and disorganized, almost formless. Some arpilleristas never finished a single quilt, and others filled their tapestries with the black or faceless figures of the disappeared, weaving in the piercing question, *¿Dónde están?* (Where are they?).

One of the arpilleristas says of her early designs, "I showed a shattered house, a destroyed building, a broken home, as my home has been since the disappearance of my son and daughter-in-law."[5] Searching for a voice, the arpillerista "told her story as she sewed, and each stitch brought us closer to her life."[6] The stitches not only commemorated lives lost but also reassembled lives that had been torn apart.

The arpilleras recounted tales of daily life under extraordinary circumstances. They

Arpillera 5: The women congregated in church basements to sew their arpilleras. The sign in the left hand corner asks, "Where are the detained-disappeared?"

called for the revival of basic human rights and denounced poverty, unemployment, food shortages, and inadequate medical care. Some honored the slain president, Allende. Others captured the day-to-day working of the arpillera workshops, the Vicaría de la Solidaridad's soup kitchens that fed the destitute, and dance classes where groups of women rehearsed folk dances.

But the subject that inspired the most memorable designs was the disappeared. Arpilleras contrasted brightly colored images of daily life with somber images of the secret police carrying out its routine of arrest, imprisonment, torture, and murder. Innumerable arpilleras bear the names and stories of the disappeared; some even include photographs of their faces—a defiant reply to the forces of silence. On the back of many arpilleras, in a little pocket, the arpilleristas inserted a message. These handwritten messages told the stories of the disappeared, adding a third dimension to the pictures on the front. These artists did all they could to keep alive the people who had vanished. To the police officers and government officials who insisted that they had no record of the disappeared and knew nothing of their fate, the artist presented a record of her own.

The arpilleras maintained the existence of the disappeared in Chile. Denied even a cross on their graves, the disappeared had memorials that also denounced the Pinochet regime. "The *arpilleras*," writes Agosín, "represent a constant dialogue with the missing . . . a thread that connects the dead with the living."[7] She explains:

> The *arpilleras* were born into a desolate and muffled period in Chilean culture, when citizens spoke in hushed voices, writing was censored, and political parties vanished. … [They] flourished in the midst of a silent nation, and from the inner patios of churches and poor neighborhoods, stories made of cloth and yarn narrated what was forbidden. The *arpilleras* represented the only dissident voices existing in a society obliged to silence. The harsh military dictatorship that stressed domesticity and passivity was disarmed [and] muzzled by the *arpilleristas*, who through a very ancient feminine art, exposed with cloth and thread the brutal experience of fascism.[8]

As time went by, the political work of these women became more sophisticated and daring—and so did their artwork. Over the years of the dictatorship, the arpilleristas revealed increasing boldness of composition and theme, and a real technical brilliance.

"AN ABSENCE OF SHADOWS," A POEM BY MARJORIE AGOSÍN

Poet and literary scholar Marjorie Agosín worked with mothers of the disappeared in Argentina and Chile. Born in Chile and raised there until she emigrated with her family to the United States, Agosín returned to Chile several years after the coup and worked with local human rights groups and relatives of the disappeared. She was among the first to meet the arpilleristas in Chile and among the first to smuggle their political artwork to the United States, spreading the story of the disappeared.

In this poem, "An Absence of Shadows," Agosín grapples with our limited ability to capture the meaning of painful and traumatic events; it focuses on the absence of the disappeared. Using metaphors, Agosín evokes feeling and images associated with the missing and with the torturous uncertainty surrounding the end of their lives. Her poem encourages recognition and communication with the disappeared, to bring them closer (if only in our thoughts). The poem struggles to find words where only fear, uncertainty, and anger exist, words that express the status of people neither dead nor alive. Its words try to fill this empty space, to anchor this experience in our hearts, and, in a way, to reintroduce the disappeared back into our communities.

I.

Beyond the shadows
where the wind dwells
among strangers,
in faraway kingdoms
clouded in fear,
the disappeared
are among the shadows
in the intervals of dream.

II.

It's possible to hear them among
the dead branches,
they caress and recognize each other,
having left behind the burning
lights of the forest
and the tapers of dawn and love.

I.

Más allá de las sombras
donde mora el viento
entre los extraños,
en las lejanías del reino
nublado del miedo,
están ellos los desaparecidos
entre las sombras
en los intersticios del sueño.

II.

Es posible oírlos entre
las ramas muertas,
entre ellos se acarician y reconocen,
han dejado las luces encendidas de la foresta
y las velas del amanecer y el amor.

III.

Beyond the province
there is an absence,
a presence of shadows
and histories.

IV.

Don't fear them,
approach them
with gentle peacefulness,
without vehemence and senseless rage.
Beyond the shadows
in the streaming gusts
of wind,
they and we dwell
in the kingdom of absences.[9]

III.

Más allá de la provincia
hay una ausencia,
una presencia de sombras
y de historias.

IV.

No les temas,
acércate a ellos
con la paz de la ternura,
sin rigor sin fuegos fatuos.
Más allá de la sombra
en las trizaduras
del viento,
moran ellos y nosotros
en el reino de la ausencia.[9]

CONNECTIONS

1. Why did the women whose family members disappeared choose to make tapestries? What were their practical and political reasons? What other ways are there to express dissent in repressive times?

2. The arpilleristas used the art of embroidery to document both their personal and political stories. What is unique about the power of visual art to tell stories?

3. Review the arpillera in this reading. What story does the arpillera tell? (Think about the colors the artist chose, the images she selected, and the arrangement of the objects in the arpillera.)

4. In the poem, Marjorie Agosín uses metaphors and images to evoke the memory of the disappeared. Why do you think she chose those metaphors (including dreams, wind, and shadow)? What can art express that other forms of documentation cannot?

5. Some believe that artists should focus on beauty and avoid politics. How can art promote human rights? What function can art have in political struggles? In education?

BEYOND THE READING

To learn more about memorials and their historical functions, go to Facing History's Internet module Memory, History, Memorials. To access the module you may also copy the following link into your browser: www.facinghistorycampus.org/campus/memorials. nsf/welcome?OpenForm.

---

[1] Marjorie Agosin, *Tapestries of Hope, Threads of Love: The Arpillera Movement in Chile* (Lanham: Rowman & Littlefield Publishers, Inc., forthcoming).

[2] Ibid.

[3] Marjorie Agosín, *Scraps of Life: Chilean Arpilleras, Chilean Women, and the Pinochet Dictatorship*, trans. Cola Franzen (Toronto: Williams-Wallace Publishers, 1987), 49.

[4] Agosín, *Tapestries of Hope*.

[5] Ibid.

[6] Ibid.

[7] Ibid.

[8] Ibid.

[9] Marjorie Agosín, "An Absence of Shadows," quoted in Marjorie Agosín, *At the Threshold of Memory*, ed. and trans. Celeste Kostopulos-Cooperman (Buffalo: White Pine Press, 1998), 237.

READING 6

The Arpilleristas: The Courage to Resist

Each month, on a given day, the *arpilleristas* would bring the tapestries they hoped to sell to the Vicaría de la Solidaridad. Since Chilean women were traditionally barred from selling the fruits of their labor, this undertaking was revolutionary. But as they entered the world of labor and politics, because they were women, the regime ignored them—arpilleristas were freer than any man in the country.

Somewhat unexpectedly, arpilleristas challenged traditional roles and male prejudices and found themselves confronting not the state but their own menfolk. In the first years of the dictatorship, remarks Morales, "men never said, 'Compañera, let's go out and struggle together to change the reality of this country.' Women were the ones who fought."[1] The men, she continues, "were so *machista*. Instead of helping us in those years, they pulled us down. Some of the women's husbands would not let them attend the meetings or help in the training or with the solidarity work."[2] Arpillerista Patricia Hidalgo echoes these themes:

> If we had stayed at home, if we hadn't participated in the workshops and everything that went on there, we would be the same as we were, we would not have grown, we would not value ourselves. I was used to having money, but I was educated like most women were, to occupy themselves with their husband and their children. To have respect and obedience and to work a lot,

but our world was always the house. When a woman begins to think and know and to believe "I am also a person" everything changes.[3]

What had begun as a search for loved ones became something quite different. The *arpilleras*, commented Agosín, "represented the empowerment of a type of domestic labor that had been considered marginal," a species of work never recognized as such—unpaid and unnoticed.[4] As they acquired this unsought power, these women encountered and resolutely faced new challenges.

Members of the arpillera cooperative came together for their own emotional and economic survival. In the workshops they discovered solidarity and cooperation and began to weave a network of support that carried them through the desperate years of the dictatorship. As their meetings became regular and frequent, they gradually added music and dancing to their group activities. This led to the creation of a dance called *la cueca sola*, popularized by the British musician and human rights activist Sting in the late 1980s. Traditional Chilean dance (*cueca*) was always performed by couples, but la cueca sola was deliberately performed alone to protest the absence of men in these women's lives. Songs and poems by the arpilleristas contributed to an increasingly distinctive women's culture. In the end, they formed roughly 200 workshops in Santiago alone.

Arpillera 6: "La Cueca Sola Chile." Created by Gala Tores, this arpillera shows women dancing a traditional Chilean courtship dance for couples, la cueca. Women danced alone to protest the disappearance of their men and gave it the name la cueca sola.

Then came the public protests. Viviana Díaz Caro, whose father was disappeared, directed the Association of Families of the Detained-Disappeared, which collected information about the disappeared and helped their relatives in the fight for justice. In this passage she recounts the political journey taken by the relatives of the disappeared in the late 1970s and 1980s:

> We completely devoted ourselves to the Association. We started to participate in the hunger strikes, chainings, street protests, and we found out what it was like to be held in jails and police stations. We weren't afraid anymore and became armed with an infinite bravery. We knew we didn't have anything to lose if we fought and our father's life was at stake. . . .
>
> Over the years, the Association initiated numerous national and international petitions asking for help in our search for victims of the dictatorship. In July of 1977 our organization wrote an open letter to General Pinochet. We accused him of being responsible for the disappearance and detention of thousands of people and asked him to tell us the fate of all our tortured relatives who were in the concentration camps. Pinochet never responded to that letter or the hundreds of individual letters that so many daughters, mothers, wives and sisters of the political prisoners wrote.[5]

An extraordinary combination of personal determination and commitment propelled the arpilleristas. Agreeing to use only peaceful methods, mothers, daughters, and sisters of the disappeared took to the streets. Their first demonstrations were nothing more than a few families and their friends collected outside Santiago's infamous interrogation centers. They marched and banged their pots around central plazas, and when the police dispersed them, hunger strikes followed, some lasting weeks.

This nonviolent strategy, which soon attracted a great deal of attention, led to a breakthrough in the search for the disappeared. Viviana Díaz Caro recalls that the "17-day hunger strike of 1978 started a powerful movement so that bishops, with the mediation of the Catholic Church,

Used by permission of Pamela Constable.

Women march on the streets with pictures of their disappeared loved ones to protest the abuse of Pinochet's power.

began legal proceedings and for the first time publicly released [their] official [records] of the detained and disappeared." The strike, she contends, "marked a milestone in our movement," drawing more people into its ranks even as it began to seek international support. Efforts extended to other Latin American countries being run as police states.[6]

> Our group helped form the Latin American Federation of the Families of Detained-Disappeared (FEDEFAM) in 1981, and our first congress was held in San José, Costa Rica. [Moreover], in 1985, FEDEFAM was recognized by the United Nations as a governmental organization. This meant we were allowed to actively participate in the United Nations Commission on Human Rights so we could denounce not only the disappearances and imprisonment, but also the serious problem of torture in Latin America. Chile held a special place in that commission because United Nations officials were sent to our country to visit detention centers [and] managed to receive information directly from tortured political prisoners. This helped us gain more support from international groups in our fight for justice.[7]

The arpilleristas played a special part in the broader struggle for international recognition. Hundreds of arpilleras were smuggled out of Chile and seized the attention of foreign audiences. Exhibitions in the United States, Canada, and France attracted thousands of viewers, and Amnesty International's colorful calendar brought images of these arpilleras to many more. While the Western media feasted on this striking art and drew attention to Pinochet's crimes, Amnesty International declared Chile's missing persons "prisoners of conscience" (people imprisoned for their political beliefs) and launched an international campaign for their release. American activists pressed their government to condemn the dictatorship and to demand that all human rights violations cease immediately. When Jimmy Carter succeeded Gerald Ford as president of the United States in 1977, his administration declared that a country's human rights record would be linked to foreign aid. To survive, Pinochet was forced to loosen his stranglehold on civil rights.

Ariel Dorfman, a celebrated writer whose role in Allende's administration had forced him to flee shortly after the coup, visited

Arpillera 7: "Where are the detained-disappeared?" This arpillera depicts the suppression of public demonstrations and contrasts the violence of the regime with the nonviolent protest of the people.

the country around that time and reported that Chileans have hesitantly begun taking over the public [spaces] of the country, gradually grouping in associations, clubs, cultural centers, trade unions, until they have managed to create a vast network of organizations outside the Government's control.[8]

Having reached a critical mass, the women's movement had allied itself with long dormant political parties to agitate for Pinochet's ouster. Dorfman felt he could pinpoint the moment when the tide turned: "It was on May 11, 1983, at 8 o'clock in the evening, to be precise, that Pinochet lost his hold over the country he has ruled for so many years." That was when "the Chilean people found a way to tell their dictator they had had enough." The nonviolent forms of protest pioneered by the arpilleristas finally resonated throughout the entire capital. "The people responded," Dorfman reported, "by banging pots and pans, blowing whistles, letting the children loose to kick up a ruckus, building barricades—and, as the noise mingled with other sounds and echoes, the powerless inhabitants of Chile discovered, with amazement, that they constituted the majority."[9]

Women returned to Chile the political voice it had lost—they did it through art, through their determination, and through the feminine symbol of the empty cook pot. Political scientist Lisa Baldez argues that in giving a political voice to the nation, the women who joined forces became a true protest movement.[10]

VIOLETA MORALES'S SEARCH FOR HER BROTHER

Newton Morales disappeared shortly after the military coup of September 1973. His sister, Violeta Morales, set aside everything else and began a tireless search for her missing brother, a search she continued until her death in September 2000. Struggling with a tradition that denied women a political role, with the repressive dictatorship, and with her own loss, Violeta recounts a story illustrating the courage and determination of many women who became artist-activists in the course of the search for their relatives.

Since the military coup on September 11, 1973, we knew that my brother would be detained. . . . After working in the industry [of electronic engineering] for several months, his co-workers at Sumar elected him president of the plant union. We in the family knew that they were looking for him because of it. On September 11, 1973, a military order was issued saying that everybody with union positions had to report to the government authorities. That is what the junta dictated immediately after rising to power. . . .

When Newton came home the men took him by the arms and he called out to my mother who was in the kitchen. "Mother, the DINA is taking me away." My mother didn't understand what was happening at the time because she had never been political. The men tried to assure her because she was grasping my brother. One of the agents took her aside and said, "Don't worry ma'am; we'll bring him back in ten minutes—we only want to speak with him. We're friends from work." My brother looked pale and didn't say anything, probably so as not to frighten our mother. . . . When they took my brother Newton away from home, my other brother was arriving and followed the wagon in his taxi. From a distance he saw them bring Newton close to the church of San Francisco, a place that we now know as Londres 38.

After our brother's disappearance, we began looking for him everywhere—like all the relatives of the detained. The DINA was created in July 1974, and the military continued refining its methods and applying them more cruelly. We began doing things immediately and found out that at the Pro-Paz Committee, which was located on Santa Monica Street, they were getting all types of reports about abuses and violations of human rights. We began looking for our brother in jails, cemeteries, morgues, commissaries, and anywhere a military regiment existed. We also went to the law courts, and at many of the places we went, they received us with machine guns just for asking questions and for going around searching for the detained-disappeared. We sent thousands of letters abroad asking for help as well. We even went so far as sending letters to the leaders of the dictatorship themselves, but nothing came of all this. . . .

My sister, my brother, my mother, and I went to Pro-Paz everyday and everywhere where we thought they could help us find our brother. . . . All of us were followed in the streets, and we were stopped and asked where we lived and where we worked. They made our life impossible. At the Pro-Paz Committee, we began organizing more and more. . . . We went to Three Alamos [a prison camp in Santiago] many times. There, the guards would ask us for things for the family prisoners, then they would give us back torn bags and would eat the food we had brought for the prisoners. Sometimes they'd tell us that visiting hours were at seven in the morning and when we'd arrive at the prison they'd say that they'd been changed to five in the afternoon; then when we returned in the afternoon, they'd tell us that the visiting hours had been on the preceding day. They were always making fun of us. On Christmas in 1974, a . . . lieutenant . . . told us that my brother was famous in that detention center. According to him they called him "Tough Guy Newton" because he tolerated the beatings well. . . . That Christmas of 1974 we asked the . . . sergeant to let us see our brother and talk with him, even if only for a few minutes. He went inside and then after a while another police officer came out and said, "Newton Morales has never been here." I had gone with my sister-in-law, who had her baby in her arms, and since we didn't leave right away, they pointed a machine gun at the child's head and told us that they'd shoot the baby if we didn't go away. . . .

Military agents also often stopped my mother near the house to threaten her and tell her that if she didn't stop bothering them searching for her son, she would also lose the rest of her children. . . . My brother Newton hadn't wanted to go into exile because he said, "I'm not leaving this country because I didn't do anything and I'm not afraid." He never imagined that in his country where the lowest of criminals has the right to a trial, he would end up without justice. He always thought that if they ever detained him, he'd have the right to a fair trial and he'd be found innocent. But here in Chile, this was not the reality. There were abuses of power by the military, which eliminated anyone who thought differently without a single law saying that thinking differently was against the law. The military made up their own criminal laws. Despite all this, we continued working with Pro-Paz and kept going on so that we could find our loved ones and fight against human rights abuses. . . .

From the despair, emerged the idea of making *arpilleras*. We didn't want to make something that would function as a decoration. We wanted to design a handmade product that would denounce what we and our country were living. We wanted to tell people about our personal experiences through pieces of our own clothing. We wanted to embroider our story, the harsh and sad story of our ruined country. At first, we had problems getting the materials, especially the cloth and the wool. So, we got the idea of cutting up our own clothes and unraveling our sweaters to make the first *arpilleras*. . . .

We opened our workshop in 1974, but we didn't go public until 1975. In those years, I took on full responsibility for the search of my brother. My sister had been kidnapped by a cab driver who interrogated her about the names of people she knew. She told him about her years as a volunteer worker in rural organizations and about all her activities as a university student. After that my sister was afraid to go out into the street to look for our brother. I was scared too. We were all afraid to keep on asking and searching. Then I put all my energy into the *arpillera* workshop; it was sometimes the only thing that kept me balanced emotionally. There I found other people who were suffering from the same thing and trying to help them sometimes helped me with my own tragedy. . . .

In the same *arpillera* workshops we started training sessions to teach the women about solidarity and their role in the soup kitchens and other group activities. Sometimes it was hard teaching the women in the townships because they treated us worse than lepers; they believed that our protest activities would put them in jail or among the disappeared. It was hard convincing them that if we didn't unite and support each other, then we wouldn't be able to do anything. Many times the money that we got from the sale of *arpilleras* paid some child's medical fees or gave relief to a workshop family member. . . .

We women of Chile who were involved in the struggle had a more difficult time because, as we now realize, our men were so *machista*. Instead of helping us in those years, they pulled us down. Some of the women's husbands would not let them attend meetings or help in the training or with the solidarity work. In those years, men never said, "Compañera, let's go out and struggle together to change the reality of this country." Women were the ones who fought. . . .

As a woman I realized as part of this process of fighting for liberty in my country that the myth that they had driven into our heads all our lives—that the man is the one with the power and physical force to control everything—only goes so far. It's relative, and it's like all the other myths that they implanted in us women. It was the women comrades who managed to end the military nightmare in our country; they had the strength that the men lacked or lost along the way. Women, who were always housewives, woke up and didn't submit until freedom returned to their country and its citizens. . . .

A few years after we *arpilleristas* organized at the Vicariate, the priest Pepe Aldunate approached us and asked us to form the group named "Sebastian Azevedo." This organization was primarily concerned with the problem of torture. . . . We were so desperate to spread our message, as so many others in our country had already done many times before, that we chose to include other art forms, such as song and dance. We not only wanted to embroider and cry out our grief, but we also wished to sing our message of protest. This is how it came about that we began organizing people in other areas to form song and dance groups. . . . Since 1973 until now, 1994, I have always worked in all of the groups whenever I could and I have organized the women in the townships. I have put my own life aside, because for all of us the Pinochet dictatorship made us exist but not live. The dictatorship forced us to renounce everything and to struggle against torture and human rights violations, as well as to search tirelessly for our loved ones.[11]

CONNECTIONS

1. What does the word *solidarity* mean to you? In what ways did solidarity and the ability to come together help the arpilleristas?

2. The arpilleras produced for the Vicaría de la Solidaridad drew on a set of traditionally female domestic skills—sewing, weaving, and embroidering, for example. In what ways were they able to turn their disadvantage as women in a traditional society into a political tool? In what ways did they defy traditional social roles in Chile?

3. In her study of the strategies used by arpilleristas and other women activists in Latin America, the feminist scholar Sara Ruddick writes about what she calls "political speech":

   > In their protests, these women fulfill traditional expectations of femininity and at the same time violate them. . . . Their political circumstances, as well as the apparently greater vulnerability and the apparently greater timidity and conventionality of the men they lived among, required that they act publicly as women. Women who bring to the public plazas of a police state pictures of their loved ones . . . translate the symbols of mothering into political speech.[12]

   Thinking about the "levers of power" available to women under the dictatorship, why do you think women were able to confront the junta more effectively than men? Why did the work of the arpilleristas lead them into conflicts with tradition?

4. What transformation does Violeta Morales's testimony document? How did the search for her disappeared brother affect her as a person? as a woman?

5. What options were available to those who hoped for democratic reforms in Chile? Why do you think the arpilleristas chose nonviolent strategies? What other nonviolent movements have you studied?

6. Why do you think human rights groups used the arpilleras to call attention to the abuses of the regime? Compare the arpilleras with the text of the document in reading 3 ("Chilean Executions"). Both document similar things. Which is more effective for you?

7. The arpilleras helped to create momentum for human rights intervention in Chile. What other ways might capture the attention of the international community? When is intervention justified?

BEYOND THE READING

The work of the arpilleristas is documented in *Threads of Hope* (Princeton: Films for the Humanities and Sciences, 1996), a film available to educators at the Facing History and Ourselves Resource Library. For more information about nonviolent political protest, see the PBS documentary *A Force More Powerful: A Century of Non-violence.*

[1] Marjorie Agosín, *Tapestries of Hope, Threads of Love: The Arpillera Movement in Chile* (Lanham: Rowman & Littlefield Publishers, Inc., forthcoming).

[2] Ibid.

[3] Ibid.

[4] Ibid.

[5] Ibid.

[6] Ibid.

[7] Ibid.

[8] Ariel Dorfman, "The Challenge in Chile," *New York Times*, June 29, 1986.

[9] Ibid.

[10] Lisa Baldez, *Why Women Protest: Women's Movements in Chile* (Cambridge: Cambridge University Press, 2002), 146–67.

[11] Agosín, *Tapestries of Hope, Threads of Love.*

[12] Sara Ruddick, *Maternal Thinking: Toward a Politics of Peace* (Boston: Beacon Press, 1989), 229.

The Chilean Struggle for Truth and Justice

In 1988 growing domestic and international pressure forced Pinochet to permit a referendum on his regime. Years of devastating hunger strikes and demonstrations had paid off. The choice was simple: a "yes" vote would extend Pinochet's rule for eight more years; a "no" would initiate a transition back to democracy. On October 5, despite scare tactics and a well-funded campaign in support of the 73-year-old dictator, the people of Chile chose democracy. On March 11, 1990, Pinochet formally stepped down and Chile began a long and painful road to democracy, truth, and reconciliation.

How important had the *arpilleras* been in ending Chile's long nightmare? The historian Peter Winn argues that during the last years of the dictatorship activists "used all means available to dramatize the plight of Chileans under the dictatorship—human rights organizations like Amnesty [International] and the UN . . . , speaking tours, media appearances and publications, musical performances—and the arpilleras." The arpilleras, "whose authenticity was very moving, [played] an important role in [this] process." They were particularly successful, Winn says, "in making Pinochet the emblematic dictator and human rights abuser of the era," and "in creating international sympathy and support for his victims and opponents."[1]

Violeta Morales (far right) holds a vigil with other women commemorating the disappeared.

When Pinochet stepped down, the Vicaría de la Solidaridad considered its job done: soon the arpillera workshops were dismantled. But although many of the weavers have since died or are now too old to weave, a new generation of artists has sprung up to continue the work begun during the dictatorship. Close to 2,000 women work under the auspices of a new organization. "The *arpilleristas* represented by Fundación Solidaridad," Agosín explains, "represent continuity, but also an extension of motives, themes and a philosophy espoused by the first arpilleristas."[2] Their political art continues to document social injustice and the arpilleras provoke discussions about how to incorporate the memory of the missing into Chile's history. These artists continue to believe in the power of women and the effectiveness of nonviolence protest. In recent years,

Arpillera 8: This arpillera symbolizes the women pushing away the wall of the dictatorship to foreshadow the beginning of democracy.

arpilleristas have not only asserted the rights of the poor to land, water, electricity, and education, they have also denounced a judicial system reluctant to punish the most bloodthirsty of Pinochet's followers.

Elsa Esquivel Rojo, whose son Luis is one of the disappeared, speaks of her anger and her need to know the truth:

> Some people say that one day we will have to learn to forgive, but I don't agree. If I knew who had taken my son, I wouldn't pick up a weapon and kill them, because I don't believe in the death penalty, but I wouldn't pardon them. . . . I would give up my home to have some kind of answer! We have to have some kind of justice for criminals, but a justice without amnesty, so that those who are responsible are punished and so that this will never happen again.[3]

As Esquivel's comments suggest, the Pinochet legacy has not been handled to everyone's satisfaction. With Patricio Alwyn, the first democratically elected president since 1973, Chile began a long and painful journey. The search for truth and justice proved frustrating and, at times, hopeless. Then Pinochet was arrested. Hopes soared. But the British magistrate who authorized the arrest in October 1998 ordered the ailing former dictator to be released 16 months later on "humanitarian grounds."[4] Late in 2005 a court in Chile finally found Pinochet fit to stand trial and cleared the way for charging him with human rights violations, tax fraud, and embezzlement. Other officials, including the notorious head of the DINA, Manuel Contreras, had already faced charges of abduction, torture, and murder.[5] But it was always doubtful that Pinochet would make it through a trial as prolonged as his promised to be. In December 2006, shortly after being placed under house arrest, he died of a heart attack in the middle of extended and complicated legal proceedings.

At the end of 2004, a commission headed by Sergio Valech, a former archbishop of Santiago, published its report on crimes committed against Chileans by the state between 1973 and 1990.* The commission recommended that a pension and health and educational benefits be granted to each of the regime's victims. President Ricardo Lagos accepted the commission's recommendations; for Chile to move forward, he felt, the state needed to

---

* Having interviewed roughly 35,000 former detainees, the commission concluded that close to 28,000 people had been detained by the military and that 94 percent of them were brutally interrogated and tortured. Some 3,400 women gave evidence; all had been victims of sexual assault or physical torture or both.

acknowledge the crimes committed in its name. He drafted a program with a resonant title: "There Is No Tomorrow Without Yesterday" (*No hay mañana sin ayer*).[6] This statement and other recently issued admissions of guilt by the Chilean military have dispelled once and for all the lies promoted by Pinochet's staff—that they knew nothing about the disappeared.

Early in 2006 Chile came full circle: a majority of the people elected Verónica Michelle Bachelet Jeria president. Michelle Bachelet's father had been punished by Pinochet's minions for serving in Allende's government. Detained and tortured, he died in prison of a heart attack. Bachelet and her mother were also detained and tortured until, thanks to connections in the military, they were deported. An independent, educated socialist in a country that until recently marginalized women, Michelle Bachelet represents many of the values the arpilleristas fought to restore.[7]

In an interview she gave at the beginning of her presidency, Bachelet reflected on the times:

I'm a completely normal woman in Chile. In fact, we have experienced a cultural shift in the last 30 years. Many women run social organizations, are union leaders, and play important roles in their children's schools. The only place where women were still absent was at the higher levels of government. . . . [As far as the disappeared go, a] country that has experienced such deep trauma as Chile can never be completely healed. I'm a doctor, so allow me to use a medical analogy to explain the problem: only cleaned wounds can heal, otherwise they'll keep opening up again, and will likely become infected and begin to fester. It's clear to me that the truth must be brought to light. Of course, there are those . . . who just want to sweep everything under the rug. In a constitutional state, the government must take steps to ensure that the judiciary can operate without obstruction. The fact that I was elected shows that Chile has a mature society. And that's why most citizens insist that no one should be allowed to place themselves above the law and escape punishment.[8]

REBUILDING CHILE:
AN INTERVIEW WITH MICHELLE BACHELET

Michelle Bachelet was elected the first woman president of Chile. Her father served under Allende's government and was imprisoned and tortured by Pinochet's secret police; he died of a heart attack in prison. Both Bachelet and her mother were also detained and tortured by the Pinochet regime, only to be sent into exile. For many, Bachelet symbolizes the radical transformation of Chile since the dictatorship. In this interview with PBS's *Online NewsHour*, she discusses the importance of forgiveness and reconciliation in the process of rebuilding trust among all Chileans:

ELIZABETH FARNSWORTH: In your speech, in your victory speech you said, "Because I was the victim of hate, I've consecrated my life to turning hate into understanding, tolerance, and why not say it—love."

As president, what policies will you follow to promote this kind of understanding and tolerance between those who tortured and killed in the past and those who were tortured, like you?

MICHELLE BACHELET: Well, I won't begin this now. I started it when I was minister of defense, and I will be doing it wherever I am until the day I will die.

It's the idea of how we're able to build bases in our society where tolerance, understanding of diversity, integration and not discrimination will be the main policies.

When I'm speaking of love, when I'm speaking of reversing hate, I'm speaking not only of reconciliation—even I don't use that word—I use another word in Spanish, that's called "reencuentro"—it's not reconciliation.

ELIZABETH FARNSWORTH: It's more a re-coming together would you say?

MICHELLE BACHELET: Yes. It's something like that because "reconciliation" is when somebody—it's related to forgiveness—and that's very individual. Some people forgive, some people do not.

So that's why I say—but let's use *reconciliation*—we will have to continue advancing in reconciliation between people who were victims and their families and people who were responsible for that. . . .

ELIZABETH FARNSWORTH: I want to talk just a little about your own situation. For example, for you, is it important that the people who mistreated you and your mother and who were responsible for the death of your father be tried? Have there been trials of . . . any of those people who were responsible for those acts?

MICHELLE BACHELET: Well, some of them—not all because, you know, we were blindfolded so we couldn't recognize who those specific persons were.

But I don't look at this as a personal issue, you know. I look at it as a process where justice must do the work and the important thing is in our country we do have trials . . . going on.

We are advancing and under my government we will still advance on three great principles: truth, justice, and reparation for all the victims, all the families of the victims.

We have been walking in that direction. And I will do all my efforts to continue in that direction. I mean—no impunity—no! Because I'm a doctor, I know when you have an injury it will heal if it's clean enough to heal; if your injury is dirty, it won't heal.

And so when you are talking in societies, we are also talking in healing processes, and for a good healing process, you need to make things right. . . .

ELIZABETH FARNSWORTH: I was really interested that night in the celebration many people said to me—even people who suffered a lot under the dictatorship— "We really appreciate the fact that Dr. Bachelet is willing to forgive."

You suffered a lot. You don't like to talk about it. Your mother was six days in a cage the size of like a square. Your father died because of the tortures—he wrote letters you've read I'm sure that are the saddest letters one could imagine, about what happened to him.

MICHELLE BACHELET: Yes.

ELIZABETH FARNSWORTH: How do you come to this position of being so positive about the possibility for *reencuentro*—the coming together of the nation?

MICHELLE BACHELET: I wouldn't be honest if I told you that in some moment of my life I [did not have] a lot of rage—probably hate—I'm not sure of hate, but rage.

But you know what happens is that then you realize you cannot do to others what you think nobody has to do to anybody. Life is important for me and not any kind of life, quality too of life.

So probably it's strange or it's difficult to understand, but everything that happened to me made me not only rationally but emotionally get to a deep conviction.

ELIZABETH FARNSWORTH: Conviction?

MICHELLE BACHELET: Yes, conviction. And that is that I have to do my best to create all the conditions in our country in order that we will be able to guarantee to further generations that they will never have to live what we had to live.[9]

CONNECTIONS

1. What do you think is the right way to address the needs and demands of people whose loved ones disappeared? If Chile is to move forward, what kind of justice should these families expect? What have other countries done to respond to the needs of victims of mass violence?

2. How can a government that abides by liberal laws cope with the legacy of dictatorial rule and massive human rights violations? Why is it important for the state to acknowledge crimes committed in its name?

3. Patricia Politzer, an outspoken critic of dictatorship and a member of the Chilean government elected after the fall of the dictatorship, described Pinochet's state of mind before his arrest in London in 1998:

   > Pinochet had taken the trip to England [primarily] for pleasure. Before departing Chile, the general and his advisors knew that legal proceedings against him were under way in Spain, but Great Britain was his favorite country, and he wanted to visit. . . . The general felt safe, and he boarded the plane to London with complete calm. He believed he had nothing to fear. Since leaving power eight years earlier, he had traveled on various occasions, and, apart from some more or less strident demonstrations by human rights groups, had not faced any mishaps.[10]

   What do you think can and should be done to fight the complacency that allowed Pinochet and other leaders accused of awful crimes to get away with it? What are the responsibilities of the international community when it comes to people who have committed gross violations of human rights? What do you think the arrest of Pinochet in England can teach us?

4. In what ways did the arpilleristas and other women help Chile move toward democracy?

5. In the interview, President Bachelet says that the process of reconciliation in Chile must start with saying no to impunity. She also refers to Chile's 17 years of dictatorship as a wound. Why do you think Bachelet emphasizes that impunity would block the process of reconciliation?

BEYOND THE READING

The last reading shows the different ways that the people of Chile came to terms with their wrenching recent history. To learn how other countries dealt with the process of national reconciliation, visit the Facing History and Ourselves online module *Transitional Justice*.

[1] Peter Winn, email message to author, February 6, 2006.

[2] Marjorie Agosín, *Tapestries of Hope, Threads of Love: The Arpillera Movement in Chile* (Lanham: Rowman & Littlefield Publishers, Inc., forthcoming).

[3] Patricia Politzer, *Fear in Chile: Lives Under Pinochet*, trans. Diane Wachtell (New York: Pantheon, 1989), 153.

[4] Peter Kornbluh, *The Pinochet File: A Declassified Dossier on Atrocity and Accountability* (New York: New Press, 2003), xi.

[5] Ibid., 482–83. We thank Peter Kornbluh for this and many other suggestions.

[6] Tom Burgis, "Chile's Torture Victims to Get Life Pensions: Report Details 'Insanity of Intense Cruelty,'" *The Guardian* (London), November 30, 2004.

[7] Jonathan Franklin, "All I Want in Life Is to Walk Along the Beach, Holding My Lover's Hand," *The Guardian Unlimited* website, November 22, 2005, www.guardian.co.uk/chile/story/0,13755,1648008,00.html (accessed February 16, 2007).

[8] "Only Cleaned Wounds Can Heal," *Der Spiegel*, March 9, 2006, Spiegel Online website, www.spiegel.de/international/spiegel/0,1518,404859,00.html (accessed March 19, 2007).

[9] "Chile's President Elect," *Online NewsHour*, January 25, 2006, www.pbs.org/newshour/bb/latin_america/jan-june06/chile_1-25.html (accessed March 26, 2007).

[10] Politzer, *Fear in Chile*, 248.

ABOUT THE PRINCIPAL PUBLICATION TEAM

Series editor Adam Strom is the Director of Research and Development at Facing History and Ourselves. He is the principal author and editor of numerous Facing History publications that are distributed, in print and online, to educators across the globe.

Dan Eshet, the primary writer of *Stitching Truth: Women's Protest Art in Pinochet's Chile*, received a doctoral degree in British history from the University of California, Los Angeles, in 1999. He taught at a number of universities, including Harvard University and Boston College. Since 2005 Eshet has been working as a historian at Facing History and Ourselves.

The author of the introduction to *Stitching Truth: Women's Protest Art in Pinochet's Chile*, Marjorie Agosín, is a human rights activist and writer, and the Luella La Mer Slaner Professor of Latin American Studies at Wellesley College, where she teaches courses in Latin American literature. Professor Agosín is recognized in both North and South America as one of the most versatile and provocative contemporary Latin American writers. She has written several books of poetry, fiction, and nonfiction, including *Scraps of Life: Chilean Arpilleras* and *Dear Anne Frank*, and she has won numerous awards for her work, including the prestigious International Latino Book Award for her book *Angel of Memory*, the United Nations Leadership Award for Human Rights, and the Gabriela Mistral Medal for Lifetime Achievement, awarded by the Chilean government.

LESSON PLANS ONLINE

Facing History and Ourselves has developed a series of lessons that accompany *Stitching Truth: Women's Protest Art in Pinochet's Chile*, which use the primary and secondary documents included in the case study to help students understand the story of the arpilleristas while revealing important insights into civil society. Included in these plans are suggestions for assessment, as well as engaging extension activities. For more, please visit *www.facinghistory.org*.

ABOUT THE MAKING HISTORY SERIES

The Making History series of case studies is part of the *Choosing to Participate* initiative at Facing History and Ourselves and illustrates how citizens as individuals and groups across the world can choose to make a positive difference in society. The historically grounded case studies illuminate what the co-chair of the Facing History and Ourselves and Harvard Law School project, Martha Minow, calls the "levers of power"—the tools available to individuals and groups seeking to fight hatred, prevent genocide, and strengthen democracy. While civic education is often limited to instruction about the basic foundations of democratic governance, these case studies reveal how the structures of civil society can be used by individuals and groups in their efforts to create positive change. Each case study highlights the challenges and legacies of people who have struggled to promote human dignity, protect human rights, and cultivate and sustain democratic values.

CREDITS AND PERMISSIONS

Grateful acknowledgment is made for permission to reprint the following: